THE DESCENDANTS OF ISHMAEL

A RELIGION OF RIGHTEOUSNESS

OR

A MARTYRS DEATH SQUAD

BY

REV. ANTHONY MARTIN

The Kingdom Culture Fellowship Ministries
&
Christian Self Publishing's

Copyright © 2015~2024 by Rev. Anthony Martin

THE DESCENDANTS OF ISHMAEL ~ A RELIGION OF RIGHTOUSNESS OR A MARTYRS DEATH SQUAD
By REV. ANTHONY MARTIN

Printed in the United States of America

ISBN 978-1-63273-026-8

All rights reserved solely by the author. The author guarantees all contents are original and do not infringe upon the legal rights of any other person or work. No part of this book may be reproduced in any form without the permission of the author. The views expressed in this book are not necessarily those of the publisher.

Unless otherwise indicated, Bible quotations are taken from
The Kingdom Culture Exploratory Study Bible
 English Standard Bible.
The Kingdom Culture Fellowship Ministries & Christian Self Publishing's

  www.thekingdomcultureblog.com

www.thekingdomculture.blogspot.com

www.amazon.com/author/revanthonymartin

Content

Preface iv
Introduction v

Part I: The Descendants of Ishmael

1. The Covenant 18
2. Al-Mahdi 52
3. A Religion of Righteousness or A Martyrs Death Squad 56

Part II: A Martyrs Death Squad

4. The Spirit of the Antichrist 90
5. Jihad 117
6. Death in the Name of GOD 125
7. Where there is Peace & Safety Disaster Strikes 130

You shall name him Ishmael,

for the Lord has heard of your depression.

He will be a wild donkey of a man;

his hand will be against everyone

and everyone's hand against him,

and he will live in complete anger

toward all his brothers."

                              Genesis 16:12

                                    TKESB

INTRODUCTION

Problems in the Middle East go back to the time of Abraham (and before if you remember the incident with the kings in Genesis 14). Genesis 16 recounts the story of Hagar and Ishmael, Abraham's other wife and child. It was Sarai's lack of faith, her impatience, which contributed to this problem. Failing to see how God could fulfill His promise of making Abraham the father of many nations, Sarai gave Abraham her hand maid. Hagar then conceived and gave birth to Ishmael. Following Ishmael's birth, the animosity between the two women increased until Hagar and her son had to leave the household. God heard Hagar's heartfelt prayer (Ishmael means "God hears"), and made the following promise in verses 11 and 12: "Behold, you are with child, and you shall bear a son. You shall call his name Ishmael, because the Lord has heard your affliction. "He shall be a wild man; his hand shall be against every man, and every man's hand against him. And he shall dwell in the presence of all his brethren." The Arab peoples today claim descent from Ishmael. The prophet Mohammed (c. 570-632 A.D.) traced his descent directly from Ishmael. In a part of the world were lineage is extremely important and where some today claim direct descent over 1,400 years from the prophet himself, there is no reason to question this deeply held conviction. Ishmael lived about 2,000 years before Mohammed, but the Biblical description of Ishmael's descendants fits. Ishmael's descendants are in constant conflict with Abraham's children through Isaac, but are also in constant conflict amongst them ("his hand shall be against every man").

INTRODUCTION

The word Arab probably has its roots in the Arabic word for "nomad." The people of Mohammed's day were nomadic. They divided into clans-tribes that fought each other continually in what is now Saudi Arabia. Mohammed was the founder of a religion that today claims almost one billion adherents. It was a combination of the traditional pagan beliefs of his nomadic ancestors, with some Judaism and a little of traditional Christianity (itself partly pagan) thrown in. At first, Mohammed's followers were told to bow down toward Jerusalem when praying. Friday was chosen as their Sabbath because it was the Jewish preparation day. None of this impressed the Jews who were hostile to the new religion. Subsequently, Mohammed's believers were told to bow down toward Mecca (a holy place in the old pagan religion), instead of Jerusalem. Mohammed's new religion was named Islam, which means "submission." Following his death, his followers spread their beliefs through conquest throughout the Middle East and North Africa, even into the Iberian Peninsula and into France. It was Charles Martel who defeated them before they reached Paris in the year 732. There were continual struggles between Catholic Europe and Islam throughout the centuries. The Crusaders pitted Catholic against Moslem for control of the "holy places" in the eleventh and twelfth centuries. Orthodox Byzantium's capital, Constantinople, founded by the Roman Empire's first Catholic Emperor in the fourth century, was captured by Moslems in 1453, one of those pivotal dates in history. Islam seemed invincible and set to expand further. It finally reached the gates of Vienna, right at the heart of Europe, in 1688-and was defeated by an alliance of Catholic powers.

INTRODUCTION

The pope at that time was present for the tercentenary celebrations of that victory in which Polish troops played a part. By this time, the Arab nations were dominated by the Ottoman Turks, fellow Moslems but not Arabs. This domination was to continue right up until this century. The Middle East has been turned on its head this century too. It is interesting to note that many Biblical prophecies about the end-time and about the Middle East in particular, could not have been fulfilled until well into this century. It is important to understand why. There are three major reasons for this sudden change in the region. First and foremost is the establishment of the modern state of Israel in the Middle East. The second major reason is the importance of oil to twentieth-century economies- and the fact that roughly half of all the world's oil reserves are in this area. A third reason is the proliferation of new nations in the area since World Wars I and II. Before we examine the background to these three major developments in the Mideast, let us look at some scriptures to fully appreciate the importance of the area in apocalyptic events. Revelation 16:16, prophecies the battle of Armageddon (literally Mount Megiddo) the final battle for mastery of the earth. This site is in the Middle East and has seen many battles fought there through history. Daniel chapter 11 also highlights end time events in the Mideast. Verse 40 says, "At the time of the end..." and goes on to prophecy a king of the north, provoked by a king of the south, sending massive military forces into the region."The Glorious Land" itself will be invaded (verse 41), while "the land of Egypt shall not escape" (verse 42).

INTRODUCTION

Interestingly, the book of Hosea talks in chapter five of an impending judgment on Israel and Judah. In verse five we see Israel, Ephraim and Judah mentioned separately. At the end of verse seven we also read that all three will fall together within the period of a new moon, which is thirty days. This has never been fulfilled before. Unger's Bible Dictionary has this to say about the captivity of the ten-tribe Northern Kingdom of Israel: "The removal of the ten tribes, though often spoken of as a single event, was a complex process.... The period during which their removal was gradually effected was not less than 150 years." The process began in 732 B.C., and was not completed until the reign of the Assyrian king Esarhaddon (681-668 B.C.). And this was just Israel. Judah's captivity "was not accomplished at once either." The first captives were taken in 701 B.C., the last almost one hundred years later in 607 B.C. Also it should be noted that there is no reference to Ephraim being taken separately from Israel, as is mentioned here in Hosea 5. This passage is revealing because it shows Israel, Ephraim and Judah all separate, but all in crisis at the same time. What must be remembered is that the modern state of Israel is only the tribe of Judah. Prophetically, although a part of Israel at this time, it is not all of Israel. It would be more accurately named Judah as it is the home of the Jewish people. Judah and Benjamin formed the kingdom of Judah, remaining loyal to David's descendants. The other ten tribes formed the kingdom of Israel. After their captivity, they disappeared. As these passages refer to events that have never been fulfilled and lead into a final captivity and national repentance in verse 15, they

INTRODUCTION

are end time events. And these end time events could not have taken place except for the creation of the modern state of Israel (Judah) in 1948. Biblically, prophetically, an independent Jewish state had to exist again. At the turn of this century hardly any Jews lived in this area at all. There were some, certainly, but for roughly 1,900 years, a Jewish presence in the area had been minimal and of no consequence historically. Suddenly, toward the end of the last century, following hundreds of years of persecution throughout Europe, the idea of a Jewish homeland began to take hold in the form of the Zionist movement. It wasn't until 1917, when British forces took Jerusalem from the collapsing Ottoman Turks, that there was ever a serious possibility of a Jewish homeland. Even then the prospects looked bleak. The British Foreign Secretary at the time, a man called Arthur Balfour, issued what became known as the "Balfour Declaration," promising the Jews their own homeland. In between this century's two world wars, Jews immigrated into Palestine while the British ruled the territory. So many came that there were riots between Jews and Palestinian Arabs in the late 20s. In 1937, a British Commission, under Lord Peel, recommended the division of Palestine into predominantly Jewish and Arab areas, with Jerusalem under international control. The United Nations recommended the same ten years later, and a few months after that the independent nation of Israel was proclaimed. Even with the U.N.'s recommendation it wouldn't have happened, except for the fact that both the Soviet Union and the United States were in agreement (this happened again in 1991 when the Persian Gulf War started).

INTRODUCTION

The Soviets saw Israel as a potential foot-hold in the area, while President Truman needed the Jewish vote in a U.S. election year. So Israel came into existence and was immediately attacked by the combined forces of five Arab nations, all determined to destroy her. With a population of only half a million at the time, surrounded by hostile peoples numbering approximately 100 million, who would have thought that Israel would survive? But it did. During the next twenty-five years Israel was to fight four major wars with its Arab neighbors, leading it to become the most powerful military power in the region-but at an incredible cost to all, not just the Jewish state itself. By 1948, rapid industrialization had made many countries heavily dependent upon oil, most of which at that time was in the Middle East. Today there are new reserves in a number of different regions of the world, but Mideast reserves are still substantial. So the whole world is easily affected by events in this area and the region is of crucial military and economic importance to the western democracies, led by the United States.

A Proliferation of Nations

Israel was not the only new country in the Middle East. Following World War I, the Ottoman Empire was divided into a number of new Arab states. Egypt had been under British domination from 1882. Iraq and Palestine came under British control between the two world wars. Syria and Lebanon were under France. Most of the Gulf sheikhdoms were British influenced to one degree or another. Kuwait was a British protectorate.

INTRODUCTION

Great Britain was the major power in the region until the late 1950s. The defeat of the Arab alliance in 1948 spread revolution throughout the Middle East. In 1952, Egypt's King Farouk was overthrown and replaced by Egypt's first native ruler for 2,000 years, Gamel Abdul Nasser. Nasser was determined to rid the region of the British and soon seized control of the Suez Canal. A resultant conflict led to U.S. intervention. The Eisenhower administration called on the British and French to leave the area, an act which contributed to the final fall of their respective empires and to American domination of the area. Nasser's radical revolutionary government tried to unite the Arabs throughout the area. In the following years, conservative monarchies were overthrown and replaced by radical young military rulers, rabidly anti-western and anti-Israel. Further attempts to destroy the nation of Israel also failed, resulting in Palestinian frustration and the growth of international terrorism. After each defeat, Arab frustration increases and violence only gets worse. This could happen again if the U.S. and Britain attack Iraq sometime in the next few weeks. The war of 1948 directly led to the radicalization of Arab politics; the war of 1956 ended the influence of the colonial powers; the Six Day War of 1967 led to international terrorism; and the 1973 war led to greater division in the Arab world as Egypt sought a separate peace with Israel. Ultimately, this led to the Palestinian uprising on the West Bank (the intifada) and also to the rise of Moslem fundamentalist violence in Egypt itself, and in some of the other countries in the region, notably Iran, which had a major anti-American revolution in 1979.

INTRODUCTION

After the next defeat, will we see another significant change? Or domestic terrorism in the U.S. and Britain? How does the current crisis in Iraq fit into this? Iraq, remember, is one of those new nations that was created after World War I. All the nations in the region are new. This means that their borders are still flexible (remember the U.S. in its first century?). There are border disputes all over. Iraq claims Kuwait as a part of its territory because they were one administrative area during the 400 year rule of the Ottomans. The British altered the border between Kuwait and Saudi Arabia in the 1920s, so Saddam was simply following in their footsteps. But Kuwait is not all that Saddam is after. He also sees himself as Nasser's successor, the man who can unite all the Arab peoples. Nasser failed to accomplish this, thereby also failing to rid the world of the Jewish homeland. Saddam was determined to accomplish both.

Complications

SEVENTEEN YEARS AGO, most Arab states were concerned enough about Saddam's ambitions to ally themselves with the U.S. in the Persian Gulf War. President Bush's diplomacy was able to line up 37 nations in military alliance, with a further twenty providing financial support. Only the U.S. and Britain were militarily involved. By any stretch of the imagination, this is a major diplomatic setback for American foreign policy.

What has gone wrong?

INTRODUCTION

Partly it's that number-one problem again-Israel. Israel has been told by the U.N. to withdraw from the West Bank. The U.S., Israel's major backer, has not forced Israel out of the West Bank, so is seen as hypocritical in trying to force Saddam to comply with U.N. resolutions. Throughout the Arab world, Israel is seen as the biggest threat to peace, not Saddam. Also, Arab leaders recognize that after the U.S. has gone, they will have to come to terms with Saddam. And Saddam was quite popular amongst the more radical elements in their countries. He is seen as a hero for standing up to the greatest nation in the world. So, even though Iraq is an aside to the main problem, it is an integral part of it. If the U.S. and Britain had made a mistake in their dealings with Saddam, it could've ignited the seventh war (to which it did) in fifty years between the Jewish state and the Arabs. To which indications were this was a part of Saddam Hussein's grand scheme and the U.S. might have inadvertently help him see the fulfillment of his dream.

To put it in a simple sentence, we may have won the war, but we lost the peace. THIS BRINGS US BACK TO HOSEA, chapter five. Here, Israel, Ephraim and Judah are all involved. The dominant nation of Israel today is the United States. Before America it was Ephraim, the multitude of nations called the British Commonwealth. Only in the last forty years has Ephraim not been the dominant power in the Mideast. But today it is the U.S. This could explain why Israel and Ephraim are mentioned separately here. Again, this could not have taken place before 1948 when the tribe of Judah came into existence.

INTRODUCTION

In verse 13, Ephraim sees his sickness and Judah his wound. What could this mean? Israel is not mentioned in this verse. Ephraim's sickness means his strength has gone. His strength was the "multitude of nations" (Genesis 48:19). Because the Commonwealth still exists and the Queen is still its head, many British people fail to realize how weakened their nation is compared to what it once was. The multitude of nations preserved Britain's freedoms in two world wars, and a number of other conflicts. For some reason, Ephraim suddenly realizes that his strength has gone. Judah meanwhile is suffering a "wound." Whereas a sickness is internal, a wound is external. This is a military setback of some kind. **Consider this scenario which would fulfill this passage.** In verse five we see Israel (the U.S.), Ephraim (Britain), and Judah (Israel today), mentioned. They all are wounded within thirty days of each other (verse 7). In verse 13 we see Ephraim and Judah going to King Jareb for help, "yet he could not heal you nor cure you of your wound."

What would lead to this?

We have a clue in the fact that Israel (the United States), is not mentioned here. For some reason the United States is out of the picture at this moment. Maybe this is the result of problems at home, or simply isolationism brought on by defeat abroad. Either of these would lead to Britain realizing its isolation. It could no longer look to the United States, its major ally, and would soon realize that its former allies, the multitude of nations, now composed of fully independent nations, is no longer

INTRODUCTION

a unified force. Judah, meanwhile, would have lost its biggest source of financial and military support. What would Britain and Judah (Israel) do? Will they go to this new super power for help-King Jareb (the Great King)? Is this the Beast (Revelation 17:13)? He is either not able or not willing to help (Hosea 5:13). Soon, seeing the weakened state of Great Britain, the United States and Judah (Israel), this European super-power invades the Middle East (Daniel 11:40-44) to impose peace upon the area. We then see the fulfillment of Christ's prophecy about gentile armies treading down the city of Jerusalem. We would also see the fall of the Jewish homeland, and the U.S. and Britain, within that period of a new moon. Events culminate in three major powers (Europe, Islam and the Far East) converging on Armageddon. This is, of course, speculative, but consider this: since 1956, when Britain, France and Israel were united in a war against Egypt to keep the Suez Canal in western hands, Britain (Ephraim) and Israel (the Jews) have had a cold and distant relationship.(Note Isaiah 11:13 in this context). It would be difficult to describe a circumstance where all three are together in some way, yet Hosea does that in chapter five, verse five. Whatever happens in the Middle East in the present and future times, keep your eyes on this part of the world. The Arab-Jewish problem cannot and will not be resolved because both sides want the same territory, particularly the city of Jerusalem and because of this passage of scripture:

INTRODUCTION

Numbers 33:51-56:

On the plains of Moab by the Jordan across from Jericho the Lord said to Moses, **51**"Speak to the Israelites and say to them: 'When you cross the Jordan into Canaan, **52**drive out all the inhabitants of the land before you. Destroy all their carved images and their cast idols, and demolish all their high places. **53**Take possession of the land and settle in it, for I have given you the land to possess. **54**Distribute the land by lot, according to your clans. To a larger group give a larger inheritance, and to a smaller group a smaller one. Whatever falls to them by lot will be theirs. Distribute it according to your ancestral tribes.

55" 'But if you do not drive out the inhabitants of the land, those you allow to remain will become barbs in your eyes and thorns in your sides. They will give you trouble in the land where you will live. **56** And then I will do to you what I plan to do to them.' "

Part I: The Descendants of Ishmael

CHAPTER I

The Covenant

Now the Lord had said unto Abram.—Heb. And GOD said unto Abram. There is no new beginning; but having briefly sketched the family from which Abram sprang, and indicated that he had inherited from them the right of primogeniture, the narrative next proceeds to the primary purpose of the Tôldóth Terah, which is to show how in Abram GOD prepared for the fulfillment, through Israel, of the prote-vangelium contained in the promise made to Eve at the fall (Genesis 3:15). The rendering "had said" was doubtless adopted because of St. Stephen's words (Acts 7:2); but it is the manner of the Biblical narrative to revert to the original starting point. Thy country.—A proof that Abram and his father were no new settlers at Ur, but that the race of Shem had at this time long held sway there, as is now known to have been the case. Your kindred.—This rendering is supported by Genesis 43:7; but it more probably means thy birthplace. It is the word translated "nativity" in Genesis 11:28. where its meaning is settled by the prefixed "land;" and the sense is probably the same here. If so, the command certainly came to Abram at Ur though most of the versions suppose that it happened at Haran. A land that I will show you.—In Genesis 11:31 it is expressly said that the land was Canaan, but possibly this knowledge was concealed from the patriarch himself for a time, and neither he nor Terah knew on leaving Ur what their final destination would be. AN EXAMPLE OF FAITH Genesis 12:1 - Genesis 12:9. We stand here at the well-head of a great river-a narrow channel, across which a child can step, but which is to open out a broad bosom that will reflect the sky and refresh continents. The call of Abram is the most important event in the Old Testament, but it is also an eminent example of individual faith. For both reasons he is called 'the Father of the Faithful.' We look at the incident here mainly from the latter point of view. It falls into three parts. 1. The divine voice of command and promise. God's servants have to be separated from home and kindred, and all surroundings. The command to Abram was no mere arbitrary test of obedience. God could not have done what He meant with him, unless He had got him by himself. So Isaiah 51:2 put his finger on the essential when he says 'I called him alone.' God's communications are made to solitary souls, and His voice to us always summons us to forsake friends and companions, and to go apart with God. No man gets speech of God in a crowd. If you desired to fill a person with electricity, you used to put him on a stool with glass legs, to keep him from earthly contact. If the quickening impulse from the great magnet is to charge the soul, that soul must be isolated. 'He that loves father or mother more than Me is not worthy of Me.' The vagueness of the command is significant. Abram did not know 'whither he went.' He is not told that Canaan is the land, till he has reached Canaan. A true obedience is content to have orders enough for present duty. Ships are sometimes sent out with sealed instructions, to be opened when they reach latitude and longitude so-and-so. That is how we are all sent out. Our knowledge goes no farther ahead than is needful to guide our next step. If we 'go out' as He bids us, He will show us what to do next.

'I do not ask to see the distant scene; one step enough for me.' Observe the promise. We may notice that it needed a soul raised above the merely temporal to care much for such promises. They would have been but thin diet for earthly appetites. 'A great nation'; a divine blessing; to be a source of blessing to the whole world, and a touchstone by their conduct to which men would be blessed or cursed;-what was there in these to fascinate a man, unless he had faith to teach him the relative importance of the earthly and the heavenly, the present and the future? Notice that the whole promise appeals to unselfish desires. It is always, in some measure, elevating to live for a future, rather than a present, and good; but if it be only the same kind of good as the present would yield, it is a poor affair. The only really ennobling faith is one which sets before itself a future full of divine blessing and of diffusion of that blessing through us, and which therefore scorns delights and for such gifts are content to be solitary and a wanderer. 2. The obedience of faith.-We have here a wonderful example of prompt, unquestioning obedience to a bare word. We do not know how the divine command was conveyed to Abram. We simply read, 'The Lord said'; and if we contrast this with Genesis 12:7, 'The Lord appeared . . .and said,' it will seem probable that there was no outward sign of the divine will. The patriarch knew that he was following a divine command, and not his own purpose; but there seems to have been no appeal to sense to authenticate the inward voice. He stands, then, on a high level, setting the example of faith as unconditional obedience to God's bare word.

The Descendants of Ishmael

Observe that faith, which is the reliance on a person, and therefore trust in his word, passes into both forms of confidence in that word as promise, and obedience to that word as command. We cannot cut faith in halves, and exercise the one aspect without the other. Some people's faith says that it delights in God's promises, but it does not delight in His commandments. That is no faith at all. Whoever takes God at His word, will take all His words. There is no faith without obedience; there is no obedience without faith. We have already said enough about the separation which was effected by Abram's journey; but we may just notice that the departure from his father's house was but the necessary result of the gulf between them and him, which had been opened by his faith. They were idolaters; he worshipped one God. That drove them farther apart than the distance between Sichem and Haran. When sympathy in religion was at an end, the breach of all other ties was best. So to-day, whether there be outward separation or no, depends on circumstances; but every true Christian is parted from the dearest who is not a Christian, by an abyss wider than any outward distance can make. The law for us is Abram's law, 'Get thee out.' Either our faith will separate us from the world, or the world will separate us from our faith and our God. The companionship of Lot, who attaches himself to Abram, teaches that religion, in its true possessors, exercises an attractive influence over even common natures, and may win them to a loftier life. Some weak eyes may discern more glory in the sunshine tinting a poor bit of mist into ruddy light than in the beam which is too bright to look at.

A faithful Abram will draw Lot after him. 'They went forth to go into the land of Canaan; and into the land of Canaan they came.' Compare this singular expression with Genesis 11:31, where we have Terah's emigration from Ur described in the same terms, with the all-important difference in the end, 'They came' not into Canaan, but 'unto Haran, and dwelt there.' Many begin the course; one finishes it. Terah's journeying was only in search of pasture and an abode. So he dropped his wider scheme when the narrower served his purpose. It was an easy matter to go from Ur to Haran. Both were on the same bank of the Euphrates. But to cross the broad, deep, Rapid River was a different thing, and meant an irrevocable cutting loose from the past life. Only the man of faith did that. There are plenty of half-and-half Christians, who go along merrily from Ur to Haran; but when they see the wide stream in front, and realize how completely the other side is separated from all that is familiar, they take another thought, and conclude they have come far enough, and Haran will serve their turn. Again, the phrase teaches us the certain issue of patient pilgrimage and persistent purpose. There is no mystery in getting to the journey's end. 'One foot up, and the other foot down,' continued long enough, will bring to the goal of the longest march. It looks a weary journey, and we wonder if we shall ever get thither. But the magic of 'one step at a time' does it. The guide is also the upholder of our way. 'Every one of them appeared before God in Zion.'3. The life in the land.-The first characteristic of it is its continual wandering. This is the feature which the Epistle to the Hebrews marks as significant.

The Descendants of Ishmael

There was no reason but his own choice why Abram should continue to journey, and prefer to pitch his tent now under the terabit tree of Moreh, now by Hebron, rather than to enter some of the cities of the land. He dwelt in tents because he looked for the city. The clear vision of the future detached him, as it will always detach men, from close participation in the present. It is not because we are mortal, and death is near at the furthest, that the Christian is to sit loose to this world, but because he lives by the hope of the inheritance. He must choose to be a pilgrim, and keep himself apart in feeling and aims from this present. The great lesson from the wandering life of Abram is, 'Set your affection on things above.' Cultivate the sense of belonging to another polity than that in the midst of which you dwell. The Canaanites christened Abram 'The Hebrew' {Genesis 14:13}, which may be translated 'The man from the other side.' That is the name which all true Christians should deserve. They should bear their foreign extraction in their faces, and never be naturalized subjects here. Life is wholesome in the tent under the spreading tree, with the fresh air blowing about us and clear sky above, than in the Canaanite city. Observe, too, that Abram's life was permeated with worship. Wherever he pitches his tent, he builds an altar. So he fed his faith, and kept up his communion with God. The only condition on which the pilgrim life is possible, and the temptations of the world cease to draw our hearts, is that all life shall be filled with the consciousness of the divine presence, our homes altars, and us joyful thank offerings. Then every abode is blessed.

The undefended tent is a safe fortress, in which dwelling we need not envy those who dwell in palaces. Common tasks will then be fresh, full of interest, because we see God in them, and offer them up to Him. The wandering life will be a life of walking with God, and progressive knowledge of Him; and over all the roughness's and the sorrows and the trivialities of it will be spread 'the light that never was on sea or land, the consecration' of God's presence, and the peacefulness of communion with Him. Again, we may notice that the life of obedience was followed by fuller manifestations of God, and of His will. God 'appeared' when Abram was in the land. Is it not always true that obedience is blessed by closer vision and more knowledge? To him that hath shall be given; and he who has followed the unseen Guide through dimly discerned paths to an invisible goal, will be gladdened when he reaches the true Canaan, by the sight of Him whom, having not seen, he loved. Even here on earth obedience is the path to fuller knowledge; and when the pilgrims who have left all and followed the Captain of salvation through a deeper, darker stream than Abram crossed, have touched the other side, God will appear to them, and say, as the enraptured eye gazes amazed on the goodly land, 'Arise, walk through the land in the length of it and in the breadth of it; for I will give it unto thee.'

<u>Genesis 12:1</u>. We have here the call whereby Abram was removed from, the land of his nativity into the land of promise. This call was designed both to try his faith and obedience, and also to set him and his family apart for God, in order that the universal prevalence of idolatry might be prevented, and a remnant reserved for God, among whom his

true worship might be maintained, his oracles preserved, and his ordinances established till the coming of the Messiah. God seems also, by sending him into Canaan, a country given up to the most gross, cruel, and barbarous idolatry, even the sacrificing of their own children to their idols, to have intended that he, and the other patriarchs descended from him, should be witnesses for God to these nations before their destruction; which is the plan God has generally, if not always, pursued; seldom, if ever, destroying a people for their wickedness, till he has sent his truth, in one form or another, and his witnesses among them. Concerning the circumstances of this call, we may receive further information from Stephen's speech, <u>Acts 7:2</u>, where we are told, 1st, That the God of glory appeared to him, to give him this call, and that in such displays of his glory as left Abram no room to doubt. 2nd, That this call was given him in Mesopotamia; and that, in obedience to this call, he came out of the land of the Chaldeans, and dwelt in Charran or Haran about five years: and from thence, when his father was dead, by a fresh command, he removed him into the land of Canaan. Get out of your country — now, by this precept, he was tried whether he loved God better than he loved his native soil, and dearest friends: and whether he could willingly leave all to go along with God. His country was become idolatrous, his kindred and his father's house were a constant temptation to him, and he could not continue with them without danger of being infected by them; therefore God said, Get out. Hereby also he was tried whether he could trust God farther than he saw him; for he must leave his own country to go to a land that God would show him; he do not say, it is a land that I will give you: nor does he tell him what land it was, or what kind of land; but he must follow God with an implicit faith, and take God's word for it in general, that he should be no loser by leaving his country to follow God 12:1-3 God made choice of Abram, and singled him out from among his fellow-idolaters, that he might reserve a people for himself, among whom his true worship might be maintained till the coming of Christ. From henceforward Abram and his seed is almost the only subject of the history in the Bible. Abram was tried whether he loved God better than all, and whether he could willingly leave all to go with God. His kindred and his father's house were a constant temptation to him, he could not continue among them without danger of being infected by them. Those who leave their sins, and turn to God, will be unspeakable gainers by the change. The command God gave to Abram, is much the same with the gospel call, for natural affection must give way to Divine grace. Sin, and all the occasions of it, must be forsaken; particularly bad company. Here are many great and precious promises. All God's precepts are attended with promises to the obedient. 1. I will make of you a great nation. When God took Abram from his own people, he promised to make him the head of another people. 2. I will bless you. Obedient believers shall be sure to inherit the blessing. 3. I will make thy name great. The name of obedient believers shall certainly be made great. 4. You shall be a blessing. Good men are the blessings of their country. 5. I will bless them that bless you, and curse him that curses you. God will take care that none are losers, by any service done for his people. 6. In you shall all the families of the earth be blessed? Jesus Christ is the great blessing of the world, the greatest that ever the world possessed. All the true blessedness the world is now, or ever shall be possessed of, is owing to Abram and his posterity. Through them we have a Bible, a Savior, and a gospel. They are the stock on which the Christian church is grafted. 6. shekem Shekem, "the upper part of the back." Here it is the name of a person, the owner of this place, where afterward is built the town called at first Shekem, then Flavia Neapolis, and now Nablous. 'ēlôn "the oak;" related: "be lasting, strong." môreh In Onkelos "plain;" Moreh, "archer, early rain, teacher." Here the name of a man who owned the oak that marked the spot. In the Septuagint it is rendered 8. bēyt-'êl, Bethel, "house of God." yam "sea, great river, west." ʿay, 'Ai, "heap."9. negeb "south." The narrative now takes leave of the rest of the Shemites, as well as the other branches of the human family, and confines itself to Abram. It is no part of the design of Scripture to trace the development of worldliness. It marks its source, and indicates the law of its downward tendency; but then it turns away from the dark detail, to devote its attention to the way by which light from heaven may again pierce the gloom of the fallen heart. Here, then, we have the starting of a new spring of spiritual life in the human race. <u>Genesis 12:1-3</u> Having brought the affairs of Terah's family to a fit resting point, the sacred writer now reverts to the call of Abram. This, we have seen, took place when he was seventy years of age, and therefore five years before the death of Terah. "The Lord said unto Abram."

The Covenant

Four hundred and twenty-two years on the lowest calculation after the last recorded communication with Noah, the Lord again opens his mouth, to Abram. Noah, Shem, or Heber, must have been in communication with heaven, indeed, at the time of the confusion of tongues, and hence, we have an account of that miraculous interposition. The call of Abram consists of a command and a promise. The command is to leave the place of all his old and fond associations, for a land which he had not yet seen, and therefore did not know. Three ties are to be severed in complying with this command - his country, in the widest range of his affections; his place of birth and kindred comes closer to his heart; his father's house is the inmost circle of all his tender emotions. All these are to be resigned; not, however, without reason. The reason may not be entirely obvious to the mind of Abram. But he has entire faith in the reasonableness of what God proposes. So with reason and faith he is willing to go to the unknown land. It is enough that God will show him the land to which he is now sent 1. Now the Lord had said unto Abram—It pleased God, who has often been found of them who sought Him not, to reveal Himself to Abraham perhaps by a miracle; and the conversion of Abraham is one of the most remarkable in Bible history. Get thee out of thy country—His being brought to the knowledge and worship of the true God had probably been a considerable time before. This call included two promises: the first, showing the land of his future posterity; and the second, that in his posterity all the earth was to be blessed (Ge 12:2).

Abraham obeyed, and it is frequently mentioned in the New Testament as a striking instance of his faith (Heb 11:8). God calls Abram from his own country and kindred to Canaan, Genesis 12:1. Promises to make of him a great and flourishing nation, and to bless in Christ his seed, Genesis 12:2, 3. Abram obeys, Genesis 12:4-6. God appears to him, and promises to give Canaan to his seed; he builds an altar, Genesis 12:7. He removes to Beth-el, and there builds an altar, Genesis 12:8. There being a famine he goes down to Egypt, Genesis 12:10. He advises Sarai to equivocate, Genesis 12:11-13. She is taken into Pharaoh's house, Genesis 12:15. Pharaoh kind to Abram for her sake, Genesis 12:16. God plagues him because of Sarai, Genesis 12:17. He calls Abram, and expostulates with him, Genesis 12:18, 19. Sends him safely away, Genesis 12:20. The Lord had said, to wit, in Ur of the Chaldees, by comparing Genesis 11:31, with Acts 7:2-4; or, did say, again, i.e. renewed the command in Haran, whilst Abram might possibly linger there, as afterwards Lot did in Sodom, longer than he should. But the former interpretation is more probable, because Moses speaks here of that command of God which came to Abram before he was gone from his kindred and father's house, and therefore before he came to Haran. And this command was given to Abram either immediately, or by Shem, then the governor of God's church. From thy father's house; from the family of Nachor, which was now become idolatrous, Genesis 31:30 Joshua 24:2; and consequently their society was dangerous and pernicious; and therefore God mercifully snatched him as a brand out of the world of fire.

The Covenant

A land that I will show you; which as yet he named not, for the greater trial and exercise of Abram's faith and patience: compare Isaiah 41:2 Hebrews 11:8. Now the Lord had said unto Abram ... In Ur of the Chaldea's, before he came and dwelt in Charran, as seems from Acts 7:2 and so Aben Ezra interprets it; but Jarchi and others think, that what follows was said to him in Haran, and so the words may be more literally rendered, "and the Lord said unto Abram"; after the death of Terah, who died in Haran; and indeed it is highly probable there were two appearances of God to Abram, and that the same words, or very near the same, were spoken to him at two several times, first in Ur of the Chaldees, and then in Haran:

get thee out of thy country; the land of Chaldea, and the city of Ur, which was in it, or out of Mesopotamia, in which, when taken in a large sense, were both Ur and Haran; and this country was now become idolatrous, for though it was first inhabited and peopled by the posterity of Shem in the time of Arphaxad, yet these, in process of time, degenerated from the true religion, and fell into idolatry. The same Maimonides calls Zabaeans, in whose faith and religion, he says, Abram was brought up, and who asserted there was no other God but the sun, moon, and stars; and these Zabaeans, as he relates from their books and annals, say of Abram themselves, that he was educated in Cuthia, and dissented from the common people; and asserted, that besides the sun, there was another Creator; to whom they objected, and so disputes arose among them on this subject:

now Abram being convinced of idolatry is called out from those people, and to have no fellowship with them; it is literally in the Hebrew text, "go to thee out of thy country"; for thy profit and good, as Jarchi interprets it; as it must be to quit all society with such an idolatrous and superstitious people: and from thy kindred; as Nahor his brother, and his family, who are not mentioned, and seem to be left behind when Terah, Abram, Lot, and Sarai, came out of Ur of the Chaldees; though it looks as if afterwards Nahor did follow them to Haran or Padanaram, which are the same, and where he continued, and therefore is called his city; see Genesis 24:10 so with great propriety Abram might be called a second time to leave his kindred as well as his country; and certain it is, Haran, or Padanaram, as well as Ur of the Chaldea's, is called by himself his country, and Nahor and his family his kindred, Genesis 24:4. and from your father's house; or household, his family, which better agrees with the second call at Haran, than with the first at Ur; for, upon the first call, Terah and his family came along with Abram, and therefore this phrase is omitted by Stephen, who speaks of that call, Acts 7:3 but Terah dying at Haran, his house or family went no further, but continued there with Nahor; only Abram and Lot, upon this second call, went from thence, as the following history makes it appear; and so Abram left, as he was bid, his father's house and family to go, as it follows: unto a land that I will show thee; meaning the land of Canaan, though not mentioned, and seems to be omitted for the trial of Abram's faith; hence the author of the epistle to the Hebrews, Hebrews 11:8

observes, that "he obeyed and went out, not knowing whither he went"; and yet it is said, that, when he and Terah came out of Ur of the Chaldea's, "they went forth to go into the land of Canaan", Genesis 11:31 and, when he and Lot went first from Haran, the same is said of them, Genesis 12:5 it is probable the case was this; there was no mention made at first what land he was to go to, and when he prepared for his journey he knew not where he was to go, but afterwards it was revealed to him that Canaan was the land, and therefore set out in order to go thither; and still, though he might know the place by name where he was to go, he might neither know the way to it, nor what sort of country it was for quality or quantity; and therefore God promises to show him the way, and direct his course right unto it, and give him a view of it, that he might see what sort of a country, and how large it was, that he would give to his posterity. This call of Abram is an emblem of the call of men by the grace of God out of the world, and from among the men of it, and to renounce the things of it, and not be conformed unto it, and to forget their own people and their father's house, and to cleave to the Lord, and follow him whithersoever he directs them. Now the LORD had said unto Abram, {a} Get out of your country, and from your kindred, and from your father's house, to {b} a land that I will show your:

(a) From the flood to this time were four hundred and twenty-three years.

(b) In appointing him no certain place, he proves so much more his faith and obedience.

The Descendants of Ishmael

1. Now the lord said] Lit. "and Jehovah said." The narrative opens with characteristic simplicity, and with the abruptness possibly indicating its selection from a group of similar traditions. the lord said] Here, as elsewhere, we must not suppose that "the word of Jehovah" was accompanied either by any external manifestation, or by an audible sound. God in old times "has spoken to the fathers" even as He speaks now to those who hear His voice, "in divers manners" (Hebrews 1:1). out of your country ... kindred ... father's house] See Genesis 24:7. The threefold tie of land, people, and home, is to be severed. Abram is to lay the foundations of the Chosen People independently of any obligation or favor due to local environment or personal association. He is to rely only on his God. Thus the first trial of the patriarch's faith requires him, (a) to renounce the certainties of the past: (b) to face the uncertainties of the future: (c) to look for and to follow the direction of Jehovah's willed. Hebrews 11:8, "by faith Abraham, when he was called, obeyed to go out ... and he went out, not knowing whither he went." the land that I will show you] The country is not designated by name: an additional test of faith. Verses 1-5, - Designed to trace the outward development of God's kingdom on the earth, the narrative now concentrates its attention on one of the foregoing Terachites, whose remarkable career it sketches with considerable minuteness of detail, from the period of his emigration from Chaldea to his death at Hebron in the land of Canaan. Distinguished as a man of undoubted superiority both of character and mind, the head of at least two powerful and important races, and

standing, as one might say, on the threshold of the historical era, it is yet chiefly as his life and fortunes connect with the Divine purpose of salvation that they find a place in the inspired record. The progress of infidelity during the four centuries that had elapsed since the Flood, the almost universal corruption of even the Shemits portion of the human family, had conclusively demonstrated the necessity of a second Divine interposition, if the knowledge of salvation were not to be completely banished from the earth. Accordingly, the son of Terah was selected to be the founder of a new nation, in which the light of gospel truth might be deposited for preservation until the fullness of the times, and through which the promise of the gospel might he conducted forward to its ultimate realization in the manifestation of the woman's seed. Partly to prepare him for the high destiny of being the progenitor of the chosen nation, and partly to illustrate the character of that gospel with which he was to be entrusted, he was summoned to renounce his native country and kinsmen in Chaldea, and venture forth upon an untried journey in obedience to the call of Heaven, to a land which he should afterward receive for an inheritance. In a series of successive theophanies or Divine manifestations, around which the various incidents of his life are grouped - in Ur of the Chaldea's (Acts 7:2), at Moreh in Canaan (Genesis 12:7), near Bethel, at Mature, and on Moriah - he is distinctly promised three things - a land, a seed, and a blessing - as the reward of his compliance with the heavenly invitation; and the confident persuasion both of the reality of these gracious promises and of the Divine ability and willingness to fulfill them forms the animating spirit and guiding principle of his being in every situation of life, whether of trial or of difficulty, in which he is subsequently placed. The miraculous character of these theophanies indeed has been made a ground on which to assail the entire patriarchal history as unhistorical. Exposition Verse 1, - Now the Lord. Jehovah = the God of salvation, an indication that the narrative is now to specially concern itself with the chosen seed, and the Deity to discover himself as the God of redemption. The hypothesis that verses, 1-4 were inserted in the fundamental document by the Jehovist editor is not required for a satisfactory explanation of the change of the Divine name at this particular stage of the narrative. Had Literally, said. In Ur of the Chaldea's, according to Stephen (Acts 7:2), reverting, after the usual manner of the writer, to the original point of departure in the Abrahamic history though not necessarily emphatic, it may be equivalent to "Go you," whoever else remains behind. Of you country proof that the date of the call was while Abram was in Ur (Calvin), though if Ur was at Edessa (vide supra) the patriarch could scarcely have been said to be from home and from thy kindred. At Ur in all probability Nahor and Milcah were left behind; at Haran, Nahor and his family, if they had already arrived thither, and according to some Terah also. And from your father's house. If they will not accompany you, no divine interdict forbade the other members of the family of Terah joining in the Abrahamic emigration. Unto a land that I will show you.... through a revelation or simply by the guidance of providence, the land itself is left unnamed for the trial of the patriarch's

The Covenant

faith, which, if it sustained the proof, was to be rewarded by the exceeding great and precious promises which follow: - according to one arrangement, seven in number, one for each clause of the next two verses; according to another, four, corresponding to the clauses of the second verse, the last of which is expanded in the third; according to a third, six, forming three pairs of parallels; according to a fourth, and perhaps the best, two, a lower or personal blessing, comprising the first three particulars, and a higher or public blessing, embracing the last three. The genealogical data in Genesis 11:27-32 prepare the way for the history of the patriarchs. The heading, "These are the generations of Terah," belongs not merely to Genesis 11:27-32, but to the whole of the following account of Abram, since it corresponds to "the generations" of Ishmael and of Isaac in Genesis 25:12 and Genesis 25:19. Of the three sons of Terah, who are mentioned again in Genesis 11:27 to complete the plan of the different Toledoth, such genealogical notices are given as are of importance to the history of Abram and his family. According to the regular plan of Genesis, the fact that Haran the youngest son of Terah begat Lot, is mentioned first of all, because the latter went with Abram to Canaan; and then the fact that he died before his father Terah, because the link which would have connected Lot with his native land was broken in consequence. "Before his father," lit., upon the face of his father, so that he saw and survived his death. Ur of the Chaldea's is to be sought either in the "Ur nomine persicum castellum" of Ammian (25,8), between Hatra and Nisibis, near Arrapachitis, or in Orhoi, Armenian Urrhai, the old name for Edessa, the modern Urfa, - Genesis 11:29. Abram and Nahor took wives from their kindred. Abram married Sarai, his half-sister (Genesis 20:12), of whom it is already related, in anticipation of what follows, that she was barren. Nahor married Milcah, the daughter of his brother Haran, who bore to him Bethuel, the father of Rebekah (Genesis 22:22-23). The reason why Iscah is mentioned is doubtful. For the rabbinical notion, that Iscah is another name for Sarai, is irreconcilable with Genesis 20:12, where Abram calls Sarai his sister, daughter of his father, though not of his mother; on the other hand, the circumstance that Sarai is introduced in Genesis 11:31 merely as the daughter-in-law of Terah, may be explained on the ground that she left Ur, not as his daughter, but as the wife of his son Abram. A better hypothesis is that of Ewald that Iscah is mentioned because she was the wife of Lot; but this is pure conjecture. According to Genesis 11:31, Terah already prepared to leave Ur of the Chaldees with Abram and Lot, and to remove to Canaan. In the phrase "they went forth with them," the subject cannot be the unmentioned members of the family, such as Nahor and his children; though Nahor must also have gone to Haran, since it is called in Genesis 24:10 the city of Nahor. For if he accompanied them at this time, there is no perceptible reason why he should not have been mentioned along with the rest. The nominative to the verb must be Lot and Sarai, who went with Terah and Abram; so that although Terah is placed at the head, Abram must have taken an active part in the removal, or the resolution to remove. This does not, however, necessitate the conclusion, that he had already been called by God in Ur.

The Covenant

Nor does Genesis 15:7 require any such assumption. For it is not stated there that God called Abram in Ur, but only that He brought him out. But the simple fact of removing from Ur might also be called a leading out, as a work of divine superintendence and guidance, without a special call from God. It was in Haran that Abram first received the divine call to go to Canaan (Genesis 12:1-4), when he left not only his country and kindred, but also his father's house. Terah did not carry out his intention to proceed to Canaan, but remained in Haran, in his native country Mesopotamia, probably because he found there what he was going to look for in the land of Canaan. Haran, more properly Charan, is a place in north-western Mesopotamia, the ruins of which may still be seen, a full day's journey to the south of Edessa, where Crassus fell when defeated by the Parthians. It was a leading settlement of the Sabians, who had a temple there dedicated to the moon, which they traced back to Abraham. There Terah died at the age of 205, or sixty years after the departure of Abram for Canaan; for, according to Genesis 11:26, Terah was seventy years old when Abram was born, and Abram was seventy-five years old when he arrived in Canaan. When Stephen, therefore, placed the removal of Abram from Haran to Canaan after the death of his father, he merely inferred this from the fact, that the call of Abram (Genesis 12) was not mentioned till after the death of Terah had been noticed, taking the order of the narrative as the order of events; whereas, according to the plan of Genesis, the death of Terah is introduced here, because Abram never met with his father again after leaving Haran, and there was consequently nothing

The Descendants of Ishmael

more to be related concerning him. The dispersion of the descendants of the sons of Noah, who had now grown into numerous families, was necessarily followed on the one hand by the rise of a variety of nations, differing in language, manners, and customs, and more and more estranged from one another; and on the other by the expansion of the germs of idolatry, contained in the different attitudes of these nations towards God, into the polytheistic religions of heathenism, in which the glory of the immortal God was changed into an image made like to mortal man, and to birds, and four-footed beasts, and creeping things (Romans 1:23 cf. Wis. 13-15). If God therefore would fulfill His promise, no more to smite the earth with the curse of the destruction of every living thing because of the sin of man (Genesis 8:21-22), and yet would prevent the moral corruption which worked death from sweeping all before it; it was necessary that by the side of these self-formed nations He should form a nation for Himself, to be the recipient and preserver of His salvation, and that in opposition to the rising kingdoms of the world He should establish a kingdom for the living, saving fellowship of man with Himself. The foundation for this was laid by God in the call and separation of Abram from his people and his country, to make him, by special guidance, the father of a nation from which the salvation of the world should come. With the choice of Abram and revelation of God to man assumed a select character, inasmuch as God manifested Himself henceforth to Abram and his posterity alone as the author of salvation and the guide to true life; whilst other nations were left to follow their own course according to the powers conferred upon them, in order that they might learn that in their way, and without fellowship with the living God, it was impossible to find peace to the soul, and the true blessedness of life (cf. Acts 17:27). But this exclusiveness contained from the very first the germ of universalism. Abram was called, that through him all the families of the earth might be blessed (Genesis 12:1-3). Hence the new form which the divine guidance of the human race assumed in the call of Abram was connected with the general development of the world, - in the one hand, by the fact that Abram belonged to the family of Shem, which Jehovah had blessed, and on the other, by his not being called alone, but as a married man with his wife. But whilst, regarded in this light, the continuity of the divine revelation was guaranteed, as well as the plan of human development established in the creation itself, the call of Abram introduced so far the commencement of a new period, that to carry out the designs of God their very foundations required to be renewed. Although, for example, the knowledge and worship of the true God had been preserved in the families of Shem in a purer form than among the remaining descendants of Noah, even in the house of Terah and worship of God was corrupted by idolatry (Joshua 24:2-3); and although Abram was to become the father of the nation which God was about to form, yet his wife was barren, and therefore, in the way of nature, a new family could not be expected to spring from him.

The Descendants of Ishmael

As a perfectly new beginning, therefore, the patriarchal history assumed the form of a family history, in which the grace of God prepared the ground for the coming Israel. The nation was to grow out of the family and in the lives of the patriarchs its character was to be determined and its development foreshadowed. The early history consists of three stages, which are indicated by the three patriarchs, peculiarly so called, Abraham, Isaac, and Jacob; and in the sons of Jacob the unity of the chosen family was expanded into the twelve immediate fathers of the nation. In the triple number of the patriarchs, the divine elections of the nation on the one hand, and the entire formation of the character and guidance of the life of Israel on the other, were to attain to their fullest typical manifestation. These two were the pivots, upon which all the divine revelations made to the patriarchs, and all the guidance they received, were made to turn. The revelations consisted almost exclusively of promises; and so far as these promises were fulfilled in the lives of the patriarchs, the fulfillments themselves were predictions and pledges of the ultimate and complete fulfillment, reserved for a distant, or for the most remote futurity. And the guidance vouchsafed (promise something) had for its object the calling forth of faith in response to the promise, which should maintain itself amidst all the changes of this earthly life. "A faith, which laid hold of the word of promise, and on the strength of that word gave up the visible and present for the invisible and future, was the fundamental characteristic of the patriarchs". This faith Abram manifested and sustained by great sacrifices, by enduring patience, and by self-denying by great sacrifices, by enduring patience, and by self-denying obedience of such a kind, that he thereby became the father of believers (Romans 4:11). Isaac also was strong in patience and hope; and Jacob wrestled in faith amidst painful circumstances of various kinds, until he had secured the blessing of the promise. "Abraham was a man of faith that works; Isaac, of faith that endures; Jacob, of faith that wrestles". - Thus, walking in faith, the patriarchs were types of faith for all the families that should spring from them, and be blessed through them, and ancestors of a nation which God had resolved to form according to the election of His grace. For the election of God was not restricted to the separation of Abram from the family of Shem, to be the father of the nation which was destined to be the vehicle of salvation; it was also manifest in the exclusion of Ishmael, whom Abram had begotten by the will of man, through Hagar the handmaid of his wife, for the purpose of securing the promised seed, and in the new life imparted to the womb of the barren Sarai, and her consequent conception and birth of Isaac, the son of promise. And lastly, it appeared still more manifestly in the twin sons born by Rebekah to Isaac, of whom the first-born, Esau, was rejected, and the younger, Jacob, chosen to be the heir of the promise; and this choice, which was announced before their birth, was maintained in spite of Isaac's plans, or that Jacob, and not Esau, received the blessing of the promise. - All this occurred as a type for the future, that Israel might know and lay to heart the fact, that bodily descent from Abraham did not make a man a child of God, but that they alone were children of God who laid hold of the divine promise in faith, and walked in the steps of their forefather's faith (Romans 9:6-13). If we fix our eyes upon the method of the divine revelation, we find a new beginning in this respect, that as soon as Abram is called, we read of the appearing of God. It is true that from the very beginning God had manifested Himself visibly to men; but in the olden time we read nothing of appearances, because before the flood God had not withdrawn His presence from the earth. Even to Noah He revealed Himself before the flood as one who was present on the earth. But when He had established a covenant with him after the flood, and thereby had assured the continuance of the earth and of the human race, the direct manifestations ceased, for God withdrew His visible presence from the world; so that it was from heaven that the judgment fell upon the tower of Babel, and even the call to Abram in his home in Haran was issued through His word, that is to say, no doubt, through an inward monition. But as soon as Abram had gone to Canaan, in obedience to the call of God, Jehovah appeared to him there (Genesis 12:7). These appearances, which were constantly repeated from that time forward, must have taken place from heaven; for we read that Jehovah, after speaking with Abram and the other patriarchs, "went away" (Genesis 18:33), or "went up" (Genesis 17:22; Genesis 35:13); and the patriarchs saw them, sometimes while in a waking condition, in a form discernible to the bodily senses, sometimes in visions, in a state of mental ecstasy, and at other times in the form of a dream (Genesis 28:12.). On the form in which God appeared, in most instances, nothing is related. But in Genesis 18:1, it is stated that three men came to Abram, one of whom is introduced as Jehovah while the other two are called angels. (Genesis 19:1) Beside this, we frequently read of appearances of the "angel of Jehovah" (Genesis 16:7; Genesis 22:11, etc.), or of "Elohim," and the "angel of Elohim" (Genesis 21:17; Genesis 31:11, etc.), which were repeated throughout the whole of the Old Testament, and even occurred, though only in vision, in the case of the prophet Zechariah. The appearances of the angel of Jehovah (or Elohim) cannot have been essentially different from those of Jehovah (or Elohim) Himself; for Jacob describes the appearances of Jehovah at Bethel (Genesis 28:13.) as an appearance of "the angel of Elohim," and of "the God of Bethel" (Genesis 31:11, Genesis 31:13); and in his blessing on the sons of Joseph (Genesis 48:15-16), "The God (Elohim) before whom my father's Abraham and Isaac did walk, the God (Elohim) which fed me all my life long unto this day, the angel which redeemed me from all evil, bless the lads," he places the angel of God on a perfect equality with God, not only regarding Him as the Being to whom he has been indebted for protection all his life long, but entreating from Him a blessing upon his descendants. The question arises, therefore, whether the angel of Jehovah, or of God, was God Himself in one particular phase of His self-manifestation, or a created angel of whom God made use as the organ of His self-revelation. (Note: In the old Jewish synagogue the Angel of Jehovah was regarded as the Shechinah, the indwelling of God in the world, i.e., the only

The Descendants of Ishmael

Mediator between God and the world who bears in the Jewish theology the name Metatron. The early Church regarded Him as the Logos, the second person of the Deity; and only a few of the fathers, such as Augustine and Jerome, thought of a created angel. This view was adopted by many Romish theologians, by the Socinians, Arminians, and others follow. But the opinion of the early Church has been vindicated most thoroughly. The former appears to us to be the only scriptural view. For the essential unity of the Angel of Jehovah with Jehovah Himself follows indisputably from the following facts. In the first place, the Angel of God identifies Himself with Jehovah and Elohim, by attributing to Himself divine attributes and performing divine works: e.g., Genesis 22:12, "Now I know that you fear God, seeing thou hast not withheld thy son, mine only son, from me" (i.e., hast been willing to offer him up as a burnt sacrifice to God); again (to Hagar) Genesis 16:10, "I will multiply thy seed exceedingly, that it shall not be numbered for multitude;" Genesis 21, "I will make him a great nation,"-the very words used by Elohim in Genesis 17:20 with reference to Ishmael, and by Jehovah in Genesis 13:16; Genesis 15:4-5, with regard to Isaac; also Exodus 3:6., "I am the God of thy father, the God of Abraham, the God of Isaac, and the God of Jacob: I have surely seen the affliction of My people which are in Egypt, and have heard their cry, and I am come down to deliver them" (cf. Judges 2:1). In addition to this, He performs miracles, consuming with fire the offering placed before Him by Gideon, and the sacrifice prepared by Manoah, and ascending to haven in the flame of the burnt-offering (Judges 6:21; Judges 13:19-20). Secondly, the Angel of God was recognized as God by those to whom He appeared, on the one hand by their addressing Him as Adonai (i.e., the Lord God; Judges 6:15), declaring that they had seen God, and fearing that they should die (Genesis 16:13; Exodus 3:6; Judges 6:22-23; Judges 13:22), and on the other hand by their paying Him divine honor, offering sacrifices which He accepted, and worshipping Him (Judges 6:20; Judges 13:19-20, cf. Genesis 2:5). The force of these facts has been met by the assertion, that the ambassador perfectly represents the person of the sender; and evidence of this is adduced not only from Grecian literature, but from the Old Testament also, where the addresses of the prophets often glide imperceptibly into the words of Jehovah, whose instrument they are. But even if the address in Genesis 22:16, where the oath of the Angel of Jehovah is accompanied by the words, "said the Lord," and the words and deeds of the Angel of God in certain other cases, might be explained in this way, a created angel sent by God could never say, "I am the God of Abraham, Isaac, and Jacob," or by the acceptance of sacrifices and adoration, encourage the presentation of divine honors to himself. How utterly irreconcilable this fact is with the opinion that the Angel of Jehovah was a created angel, is conclusively proved by Revelation 22:9, which is generally regarded as perfectly corresponding to the account of the "Angel of Jehovah" of the Old Testament. The angel of God, who shows the sacred seer the heavenly Jerusalem, and who is supposed to say, "Behold, I come quickly" (Revelation 22:7), and "I am Alpha and

Omega" (Revelation 22:13), refuses in the most decided way the worship which John is about to present, and exclaims, "See I am thy fellow-servant: worship God." Thirdly, the Angel of Jehovah is also identified with Jehovah by the sacred writers themselves, who call the Angel Jehovah without the least reserve (cf. Exodus 3:2 and Exodus 3:4, Judges 6:12 and Judges 6:14-16, but especially Exodus 14:19, where the Angel of Jehovah goes before the host of the Israelites, just as Jehovah is said to do in Exodus 13:21). - On the other hand, the objection is raised, that in the New Testament, which is confessedly the Greek rendering of is always a created angel, and for that reason cannot be the uncreated Logos or Son of God, since the latter could not possibly have announced His own birth to the shepherds at Bethlehem. But this important difference has been overlooked, that according to Greek usage, denotes an (any) angel of the Lord, whereas according to the rules of the Hebrew language means the angel of the Lord; that in the New Testament the angel who appears is always described as without the article, and the definite article is only introduced in the further course of the narrative to denote the angel whose appearance has been already mentioned, whereas in the Old Testament it is always "the Angel of Jehovah" who appears, and whenever the appearance of a created angel is referred to, he is introduced first of all as "an angel" (1 Kings 19:5 and 1 Kings 19:7).

At the same time, it does not follow from this use of the expression Maleach Jehovah that the (particular) angel of Jehovah was essentially one with God, or that Maleach Jehovah always has the same signification; for in Malachi 2:7 the priest is called Maleach Jehovah, i.e., the messenger of the Lord. Who the messenger or angel of Jehovah was, must be determined in each particular instance from the connection of the passage; and where the context furnishes no criterion, it must remain undecided. Consequently such passages as Psalm 34:7; Psalm 35:5-6, etc., where the angel of Jehovah is not more particularly described, or Numbers 20:16, where the general term angel is intentionally employed, or Acts 7:30; Galatians 3:19, and Hebrews 2:2, where the words are general and indefinite, furnish no evidence that the Angel of Jehovah, who proclaimed Himself in His appearances as one with God, was not in reality equal with God, unless we are to adopt as the rule for interpreting Scripture the inverted principle, that clear and definite statements are to be explained by those that are indefinite and obscure. In attempting now to determine the connection between the appearance of the Angel of Jehovah (or Elohim) and the appearance of Jehovah or Elohim Himself, and to fix the precise meaning of the expression Maleach Jehovah, we cannot make use, as recent opponents of the old Church view have done, of the manifestation of God in Genesis 18 and 19, and the allusion to the great prince Michael in Daniel 10:13, Daniel 10:21; Daniel 12:1; just because neither the appearance of Jehovah in the former instance, nor that of the archangel Michael in the latter, is represented as an appearance of the Angel of Jehovah.

We must confine ourselves to the passages in which "the Angel of Jehovah" is actually referred to. We will examine these, first of all, for the purpose of obtaining a clear conception of the form in which the Angel of Jehovah appeared. Genesis 16, where He is mentioned for the first time, contains no distinct statement as to His shape, but produces on the whole the impression that He appeared to Hagar in a human form, or one resembling that of man; since it was not till after His departure that she drew the inference from His words, that Jehovah had spoken with her. He came in the same form to Gideon, and sat under the terebinth at Ophrah with a staff in His hand (Judges 6:11 and Judges 6:21); also to Manoah's wife, for she took Him to be a man of God, i.e., a prophet, whose appearance was like that of the Angel of Jehovah (Judges 13:6); and lastly, to Manoah himself, who did not recognize Him at first, but discovered afterwards, from the miracle which He wrought before his eyes, and from His miraculous ascent in the flame of the altar, that He was the Angel of Jehovah (Judges 13:9-20). In other cases He revealed Himself merely by calling and speaking from heaven, without those who heard His voice perceiving any form at all; e.g., to Hagar, in Genesis 21:17., and to Abraham, Genesis 22:11. On the other hand, He appeared to Moses (Exodus 3:2) in a flame of fire, speaking to him from the burning bush, and to the people of Israel in a pillar of cloud and fire (Exodus 14:19, cf. Exodus 13:21.), without any angelic form being visible in either case. Balaam He met in a human or angelic form, with a drawn sword in His hand (Numbers 22:22-23). David saw Him by the threshing-floor of Araunah, standing between heaven and earth, with the sword drawn in His hand and stretched out over Jerusalem (1 Chronicles 21:16); and He appeared to Zechariah in a vision as a rider upon a red horse (Zechariah 1:9.). - From these varying forms of appearance it is evident that the opinion that the Angel of the Lord was a real angel, a divine manifestation, "not in the disguise of angel, but through the actual appearance of an angel," is not in harmony with all the statements of the Bible. The form of the Angel of Jehovah, which was discernible by the senses, varied according to the purpose of the appearance; and, apart from Genesis 21:17 and Genesis 22:11, we have a sufficient proof that it was not a real angelic appearance, or the appearance of a created angel, in the fact that in two instances it was not really an angel at all, but a flame of fire and a shining cloud which formed the earthly substratum of the revelation of God in the Angel of Jehovah (Exodus 3:2; Exodus 14:19), unless indeed we are to regard natural phenomena as angels, without any scriptural warrant for doing so. The only passage that could be adduced in support of this, viz., Psalm 104:4, does not prove that God makes natural objects, winds and flaming fire, into forms in which heavenly spirits appear, or that He creates spirits out of them. Even if we render this passage, is not to the creation of angels; nor can the meaning be, that God gives wind and fire to His angels as the material of their appearance, and as it were of their self-incorporation.

For constructed with two accusatives, the second of which expresses the material is never met with in this sense, not even in 2 Chronicles 4:18-22. For the greater part of the temple furniture summed up in this passage, of which it is stated that Solomon made them of gold, was composed of pure gold.

CHAPTER II

Al-MAHDI

"More than one hundred Hadiths were narrated about Al-Mahdi. Those Hadiths ranged between being fabricated, weak, sound, and authentic; the authentic ones are very few of such Hadiths are the following:

1. `Ali Ibn Abi Talib quoted the Prophet (peace and blessings be upon him) as saying: **"Al-Mahdi is one of us, the clan of the Prophet (peace and blessings be upon him). Allah will reform him in one night."**

2. There were three Hadiths narrated on the authority of Abu Sa`id Al-Kudri (may Allah be pleased with him). Such Hadiths were reported by Al-Hakim; and some of them were reported by Abu Dawud, At-Tirmidhi, Ibn Maqah, Imam Ahmad, and others. Of these Hadiths, At-Tirmidhi reported that the Prophet said: **"Al-Mahdi is from my Ummah; he will be born and live to rule five or seven or nine years. (If) one goes to him and says: 'Give me (a charity), he will fill one's garment with what one needs.'"**

3. Abu Dawud also reported a Hadith about Al-Mahdi that the Prophet (peace and blessings be upon him) said: **"Al-Mahdi will be of my stock, and will have a broad forehead, a prominent nose.**

He will fill the earth with equity and justice as it was filled with oppression and tyranny, and he will rule for seven years." 4. There is also the Hadith narrated by Thawban (may Allah be pleased with him) in which the Prophet (peace and blessings be upon him) said: **"If you see the black banners emerging from Khurasan, seek to join their supporters even if creeping, because among them will be caliph Al-Mahdi."** That Hadith was reported by Al-Hakim and Ahmad. But the chains of narration of that hadith were all unauthentic, though some Hadith scholars rendered it sound in general. Some people stated that the aforementioned Hadith is cited to support that Al-Mahdi will emerge from among the Abbasid State. That Hadith might be fabricated altogether or its words might be distorted so as to support the Abbasid State. Added to the above, that there are Hadiths reported about Al-Mahdi that are true in general, but most of them do not reach the degree of authenticity. It may be only one of these Hadiths that is regarded authentic. Moreover, it is only a few of them that are considered sound, while most of them are weak. Many scholars tackled the subject of Al-Mahdi, among whom was Na`im Ibn Hamad. He wrote about Al-Mahdi in his book *Al-Fitan*. Although Maim was an Imam of Sunni, Ad-Darqatani, Adh-Dhahabi and Ibn Hajar mentioned that there were some weak and fabricated Hadiths reported. Others who wrote about Al-Mahdi are Abu Na`im Al-Asfahani and Yusuf Ibn Yahyah As-Salami, whose book is named *"`Uqad Ad-Durar*. Ibn Khaldun also wrote about that subject in his well-known book *Al-Muqaddimah*.

He stated: "It is known among the majority of Muslims that Al-Mahdi is a fact." He further stated that the majority of scholars and Imams emphasized the Hadiths reported about Al-Mahdi in general, though many of these Hadiths were controversial. There are also many recent scholars who believed in the truthfulness of the Hadiths reported about Al-Mahdi in general. However, some scholars denied all the Hadiths reported in that regard. Of those scholars was Mujahid, who claimed that Al-Mahdi would be Jesus, Son of Mary. In that respect, Ibn Maqah and Al-Hakim reported a weak Hadith to the effect that Al-Mahdi would be Jesus, Son of Mary. Among the recent scholars who believe the Hadiths about Al-Mahdi in general are Sheikh Muhammad Rashid Rida, Sheikh `Abdullah bin Zayd Aal-Mahmud, Muhammad Muhi Ad-Din `Abdul-Hamid and others Muslims who are of Ahl-us Sunnah (mainstream Muslims) believe that a man of the Prophet's clan will be born before the end of this world and lead an ordinary life as any other one; he may commit mistakes and will need to be reformed like any other one. Then Allah will choose him to reunite the Muslims and guide them to the right path. This is all what should be believed about Al-Mahdi. There is no religious text to the effect that it is a religious duty to wait anxiously for him. Moreover, Muslims should not believe anyone claiming that he is Al-Mahdi unless there is clear evidence to that effect, as many people have claimed to be so. Thus, Muslims are required not to hasten to believe anyone claiming to be Al-Mahdi; they are to investigate and make sure of such a thing. There is no ruling in the Islamic Shari`ah that has to do with the emergence of Al-Mahdi.

That is to say, Muslims are not to delay fulfilling religious duties like the congregational prayers or Jihad or applying penalties prescribed in Shari`ah, etc., until Al-Mahdi comes and guides them in that respect. Muslims are to lead their lives normally — worship Allah, go to work, reform their society, learn, teach, etc., and if Al-Mahdi appears and they make sure that he is truthful, they are to follow him. This was the attitude of the Companions and those who truly followed in their footsteps."

CHAPTER III

A Religion of Righteousness or A Martyrs Death Squad

And I saw thrones, and they sat . . . There is a prominence given to the thrones, because the thought of the reign of the saints is uppermost in the mind of the seer. The thrones are seen, and those who sat on them. It has been asked, "By whom are the thrones occupied?" The answer is supplied in the latter part of the verse. Those who are in the latter part said to reign with Christ are clearly those who sit upon the thrones which first caught the prophet's eye; these are all the real servants of God. They appear before the seer in two great classes:— First, the martyrs who have been faithful unto death; for he speaks first of seeing the souls of those who have been beheaded (strictly, "slain with the axe," but clearly the special class of beheaded martyrs is to be taken as representing all), because of the testimony of Jesus, and because of the word of God. The number of the martyrs is now complete (comp. Revelation 6:11); these form the first class mentioned. Secondly, those who have been faithful in life occupy these thrones. The prophet sees these, even whosoever did not worship (during life) the wild beast, nor yet his image, and did not receive the mark (Revelation 13:10) on their forehead and upon their hand. The triumph and sovereignty, whatever they be, are shared by all the faithful. These things are stated as constituting their privileges. They lived, whereas the rest of the dead lived not; they reigned, and judgment was given them. This last has been felt to be a difficulty.

The Descendants of Ishmael

What sort of judgment is intended? The passage in Daniel (Daniel 7:22) is clearly suggestive of the present one. The phrase (judgment was given) is not there to be understood as meaning that right was done them (see Note in Speaker's Commentary on Daniel), neither must it be so understood here. Judicial powers are given to the saints as to those who occupy thrones; "the chief power in governing" is given them (comp. Matthew 19:28, and 1Corinthians 6:2-3); they reign, they judge, they live; the true and full powers of life are seen to be theirs. And is not this the case always? Who, next to Him who knows the secrets of our hearts, exercises judicial powers over men? Do not those whose lives, as we read them, rebuke our own? Truly, those who lived for God, and refused the mark of earthliness, reign and judge us in our worldliness and weakness. This is their sovereign honor here, besides the glad reign in the unseen world Revelation 20:4-6. And I saw thrones — Such as were promised to the apostles, Matthew 19:28; Luke 22:30; and they — Namely, the saints, whom St. John saw at the same time; sat upon them, and judgment was given to them — 1 Corinthians 6:2. Error and sin being restrained, the reign of righteousness succeeds, and the administration of justice and judgment is given to the saints of the Most High, Daniel 7:22. And I saw the souls — That is, the persons; of them that were beheaded — Namely, with the axe, as the word properly signifies: one kind of death, however, which was particularly inflicted at Rome, is mentioned for all kinds thereof: for the witness, or testimony, of Jesus — For testifying that Jesus of Nazareth is the true Messiah, the Son of God, the Savior, Lawgiver, and

A Religion of Righteousness or A Martyrs Death Squad

final Judge of the world, and especially of those who believe in him; and for the word of God — In general, or for some particular and peculiarly important truth of it; or for bearing witness to the great truths of the everlasting gospel; and who had not worshipped the beast — Had not made any acknowledgment of subjection to the antichristian power of the beast, nor yielded to the prevailing corruptions; nor his image — The pope and his corrupt hierarchy; but had persevered in the true Christian faith against all opposition. See on Revelation 13:4-8; Revelation 13:11-17. Neither had received his mark in their foreheads, or on their hands — Had neither made an open profession of his corrupt religion, nor had secretly complied with its idolatries or superstitions. And they lived — Their souls and bodies being reunited; and reigned with Christ — It is not said, on earth. Doubtless the meaning is that they ascended and reigned with him in heaven; a thousand years — Namely, before the rest of the dead, even the one thousand years during which Satan is bound, and truth and righteousness prevail over all the earth. Although the martyrs, when thus raised from the dead, shall not continue on earth, it is highly probable that, in proof of their resurrection, they will appear to pious individuals, in the places where they were so cruelly martyred, and where they are raised: as those saints who, at Jerusalem, rose with Christ, went into the city, and appeared to many, Matthew 27:52-53. And if so, it is likely this circumstance will tend greatly to confirm the faith and hope of believers respecting the resurrection of the dead, and will check vice and profaneness, and contribute much to the spread of the gospel. "The martyrs and confessors of Jesus," says Bishop Newton, "who are here represented as being raised from the dead, at least one thousand years before others, are not only those who were beheaded, or suffered any kind of death, under the heathen Roman emperors, but also those who refused to comply with the idolatrous worship of the beast and his image. All these have this peculiar prerogative above the rest of mankind: they all share in this first resurrection. And all of them the apostle here pronounces, Blessed and holy is he that hath part in the first resurrection — He is holy in all senses of the word: holy, as separated from the common lot of mankind; holy, as endowed with all virtuous qualifications; and none but such are admitted to partake of this blessed state. On such the second death has no power — The second death is a Jewish phrase for the punishment of the wicked after death. The Chaldea paraphrase of Onkelos, and the other paraphrases of Jonathan Ben Uzziel, and of Jerusalem, on Deuteronomy 33:6, Let Reuben live, and not die, say, Let him not die the second death, by which the wicked die in the world to come. The sons of the resurrection, therefore, shall not die again, but shall live in eternal bliss, and be priests of God and Christ, and reign with him a thousand years" — Before any others. For the Lord Jesus will not suffer any of his disciples to be, in the end, losers for their fidelity to him and his cause. These loved not their lives unto death, but voluntarily sacrificed them out of love to him; and he thus amply recompenses them. He gives each of them an infinitely better life than that given up for his sake

A Religion of Righteousness or A Martyrs Death Squad

— and this a thousand years before the other pious dead receive theirs. "Nothing is more evident," says Bishop Newton, "than that this prophecy of the millennium, and of the first resurrection, hath not yet been fulfilled, even though the resurrection be taken in a figurative sense. For reckon the thousand years from the time of Christ, or reckon them from the time of Constantine, yet neither of these periods, nor indeed any other, will answer the description and character of the millennium, the purity and peace, the holiness and happiness of that blessed state. Before Constantine, indeed, the church was in greater purity; but was groaning under the persecutions of the heathen emperors. After Constantine, the church was in greater prosperity, but was soon shaken and disturbed by heresies and schisms, by the incursions and devastations of the northern nations, by the conquering arms and prevailing imposture of the Saracens, and afterward of the Turks; by the corruption, idolatry, and wickedness — the usurpation, tyranny, and cruelty, of the Church of Rome. If Satan was then bound, when can he be said to be loosed? Or how could the saints and the beast, Christ and antichrist, reign at the same period? This prophecy therefore remains to be fulfilled, even though the resurrection be taken only for an allegory, which yet the text cannot admit without the greatest torture and violence. For with what propriety can it be said, that some of the dead, who were beheaded, lived and reign with Christ a thousand years, but the rest of the dead lived not again until the thousand years were finished, unless the dying and living again be the same in both places a proper death and resurrection? Indeed the death and resurrection of the witnesses before mentioned, chap. 11., appears, from the concurrent circumstances of the vision, to be figurative; but the death and resurrection here mentioned must, for the very same reasons, be concluded to be real. If the martyrs rise only in a spiritual sense, then the rest of the dead rise only in a spiritual sense; but if the rest of the dead really rise, the martyrs rise in the same manner. There is no difference between them: and we should be cautious and tender of making the first resurrection an allegory, lest others should reduce the second into an allegory too, like those whom St. Paul mentions 2 Timothy 2:17-18. In the general, that there shall be such a happy period is the plain and express doctrine of Daniel 7:27; Psalm 2:8; Isaiah 11:9; Romans 11:25-26, and of all the prophets, as well as of St. John; and we daily pray for the accomplishment of it in saying, Thy kingdom come. But, of all the prophets, St. John is the only one who hath declared particularly, and in express terms, that the martyrs shall rise at the commencement of it, though, as has been observed, probably not to remain on earth, but to ascend and be with Christ in heaven; and that this happy state of the church shall continue for one thousand years. And the Jewish Church before him, and the Christian Church after him, have further believed and taught that these thousand years will be the seventh millenary of the world. A pompous heap of quotations might be produced to this purpose, both from Jewish and Christian writers; but to enumerate only a few of both sorts: among the Jewish writers

A Religion of Righteousness or A Martyrs Death Squad

are, Rabbi Katina, and the house of Elias; among the Christian writers are, St. Barnabas in the first century, Justin Martyr in the second century, Tertullian in the beginning of the third, and Lactantius in the beginning of the fourth century. In short, the doctrine of the millennium was generally believed in the first three and purest ages of the church: and this belief was one principal cause of the fortitude of the primitive Christians: they even coveted martyrdom, in hopes of being partakers of the privileges and glories of the martyrs in the first resurrection. Afterward, this doctrine grew into disrepute, for various reasons. Some, both Jewish and Christian writers have debased it with a mixture of fables. It has suffered by the misrepresentations of its enemies, as well as by the indiscretions of its friends; it has been abused to the worst purposes: it has been made an engine of faction. Besides, wherever the influence and authority of the Church of Rome have extended, she hath endeavored by all means to discredit this doctrine; and, indeed, not without sufficient reason, this kingdom of Christ being founded on the ruins of antichrist. No wonder, therefore, that this doctrine lay depressed for many ages; but it sprang up again at the Reformation, and will flourish together with the study of the Revelation. All the danger is, on the one side, of pruning and lopping it too short; and, on the other, of suffering it to grow too wild and luxuriant. Great caution and judgment are required to keep in the middle way. We should neither, with some, interpret into an allegory; nor, with others, indulge an extravagant fancy, nor explain too curiously the manner and circumstances of this future state. We must not imagine that the appearance of Christ, to introduce this glorious state of the church, will be a personal one, any more than his appearance to destroy Jerusalem, and punish the Jewish nation by Titus, was such; for the heavens must retain him until the time of the restitution of all things. Nor are we to imagine that, in this prosperous state of the church, it shall be free from all mixture of hypocrisy, error, and sin, seeing that the sudden and general apostasy which will follow that period shows that all were not Israel that feigned themselves to be of it; otherwise it is not likely that God, in his equity and goodness, would suffer the enemies of his people so dreadfully to assault them as they are here represented to do. It is safest and best faithfully to adhere to the words of Scripture, and to rest contented with the general account, till time shall accomplish all the particulars. 20:4-6 Here is an account of the reign of the saints, for the same space of time as Satan is bound. Those who suffer with Christ shall reign with him in his spiritual and heavenly kingdom, in conformity to him in his wisdom, righteousness, and holiness: this is called the first resurrection, with which none but those who serve Christ, and suffer for him, shall be favored. The happiness of these servants of God is declared. None can be blessed but those that are holy; and all that are holy shall be blessed. We know something thing of what the first death is, and it is very awful; but we know not what this second death is.

A Religion of Righteousness or A Martyrs Death Squad

It must be much more dreadful; it is the death of the soul, eternal separation from God. May we never know what it is: those who have been made partakers of a spiritual resurrection are saved from the power of the second death. We may expect that a thousand years will follow the destruction of the antichristian, idolatrous, persecuting powers, during which pure Christianity, in doctrine, worship, and holiness, will be made known over all the earth. By the all-powerful working of the Holy Spirit, fallen man will be new-created; and faith and holiness will as certainly prevail, as unbelief and unholiness now do. We may easily perceive what a variety of dreadful pains, diseases, and other calamities would cease, if all men were true and consistent Christians. All the evils of public and private contests would be ended, and happiness of every kind largely increased. Every man would try to lighten suffering, instead of adding to the sorrows around him. It is our duty to pray for the promised glorious days, and to do everything in our public and private stations which can prepare for that. And I saw thrones - Revelation 1:4; Rev 3:21; 4:3-4. John here simply says, that he saw in vision thrones, with persons sitting on them, but without entreating who they were that sat on them. It is not the throne of God that is now revealed, for the word is in the plural number, though the writer does not hint how "many" thrones there were. It is intimated, however, that these thrones were placed with some reference to pronouncing a judgment, or determining the destiny of some portion of mankind, for it is immediately added, "And judgment was given to them."

There is considerable resemblance, in many respects, between this and the statement in Daniel 7:9; "I beheld until the thrones were cast down, and the Ancient of days did sit"; or, as it should be rendered, "I beheld" - that is, I continued to look - "until the thrones were placed or set," to wit, for the purposes of judgment. John here sees, as the termination of human affairs approaches, thrones placed with reference to a determination of the destiny of some portion of the race, "as if" they were now to have a trial, and to receive a sentence of acquittal or condemnation. The "persons" on whom this judgment is to pass are specified, in the course of the verse, as those who were "beheaded for the witness of Jesus, who had the Word of God, who had not worshipped the beast," etc. The "time" when this was to occur manifestly was at the Beginning of the thousand years. And they sat upon them - Who sat on them is not mentioned. The natural construction is that "judges" sat on them, or that persons sat on them to whom judgment was entrusted. The language is such as would be used on the supposition either that he had mentioned the subject before, so that he would be readily understood, or that, from some other cause, it was so well understood that there was no necessity for mentioning who they were. John seems to have assumed that it would be understood who were meant. And yet to us it is not entirely clear; for John has not before this given us any such intimation that we can determine with certainty what is intended. The probable construction is that those are referred to whom it appropriately belonged to occupy such seats of judgment, and who they are is to be determined from other parts of the Scriptures. In Matthew 19:28, the Savior says to his apostles, "When the Son of man shall sit on the throne of his glory, ye also shall sit upon twelve thrones, judging the twelve tribes of Israel." In 1 Corinthians 6:2, Paul asks the question, "Do you not know that the saints shall judge the world?" The meaning as thus explained is, that Christians will, in some way, be employed in judging the world; that is, that they will be exalted to the right hand of the Judge, and be elevated to a station of honor, as if they were associated with the Son of God in the judgment. Something of that kind is, doubtless, referred to here; and John probably means to say that he saw the thrones placed on which those will sit who will be employed in judging the world. If the apostles are specially referred to, it was natural that John, eminent for modesty, should not particularly mention them, as he was one of them, and as the true allusion would be readily understood. And judgment was given unto them - The power of pronouncing sentence in the case referred to be conferred on them, and they proceeded to exercise that power. This was not in relation to the whole race of mankind, but to the martyrs, and to those who, amidst many temptations and trials, had kept themselves pure. The sentence which is to be passed would seem to be that in consequence of which they are to be permitted to "live and reign with Christ a thousand years." The "form" of this expressed approval is that of a resurrection and judgment; whether this is the "literal" mode is another inquiry, and will properly be considered when the exposition of the passage shall have been given. And I saw the souls of them - This is a very important expression in regard to the meaning of the whole passage. John says he saw "the souls" - not "the bodies." If the obvious meaning of this be the correct meaning; if he saw the "souls" of the martyrs, not the "bodies," this would seem to exclude the notion of a "literal" resurrection, and consequently overturn many of the theories of a literal resurrection, and of a literal reign of the saints with Christ during the thousand years of the millennium. The doctrine of the last resurrection, as everywhere stated in the Scripture, is, that the "body" will be raised up, and not merely that the "soul will live" (see 1 Corinthians 15, and the notes on that chapter); and consequently John must mean to refer in this place to something different from that resurrection, or to "any" proper resurrection of the dead as the expression is commonly understood. The doctrine which has been held, and is held, by those who maintain that there will be a "literal resurrection" of the saints to reign with Christ during a thousand years; can receive no support from this passage, for there is no ambiguity respecting the word "souls" - ψυχὰς psuchas - as used here. By no possible construction can it mean the "bodies" of the saints. If John had intended to state that the saints, as such, would be raised as they will be at the last day, it is clear that he would not have used this language, but would have employed the common language of the New Testament to denote it.

A Religion of Righteousness or A Martyrs Death Squad

The language here does not express the doctrine of the resurrection of the body; and if no other language but this had been used in the New Testament, the doctrine of the resurrection, as now taught and received, could not be established. These considerations make it clear to my mind that John did not mean to teach that there would be a literal resurrection of the saints, that they might live and reign with Christ personally during the period of a thousand years. There was undoubtedly something that might be "compared" with the resurrection, and that might, in some proper sense, is "called" a resurrection Revelation 20:5-6, but there is not the slightest notion that it would be a resurrection of the "body,"(a renewed body) or that it would be identical with the "final" resurrection. John undoubtedly intends to describe some honor conferred on the "spirits or souls" of the saints and martyrs during this long period, as if they were raised from the dead, or which might be represented by a resurrection from the dead. What that honor is to be, is expressed by their "living and reigning with Christ." The meaning of this will be explained in the exposition of these words; but the word used here is fatal to the notion of a literal resurrection and a personal reign with Christ on the earth. That were beheaded - The word used here - πελεκίζω pelekizō - occurs nowhere else in the New Testament. It properly means, "to axe," that is, to hew or cut with an axe - from πέλεκυς pelekus, "axe." Hence it means to behead with an axe. This was a common mode of execution among the Romans, and doubtless many of the Christian martyrs suffered in this manner; but "it cannot be supposed to have been the intention of the writer to confine the rewards of martyrs to those who suffered in this particular way; for this specific and ignominious method of punishment is designated merely as the symbol of any and every kind of martyrdom". For the witness of Jesus - As witnesses of Jesus; or bearing in this way their testimony to the truth of his religion. Revelation 1:9; Revelation 6:9. And for the Word of God - Revelation 1:9, "Which had not worshipped the beast." Who had remained faithful to the principles of the true religion, and had resisted all the attempts made to seduce them from the faith, even the temptations and allurements in the times of the papacy. See this language explained in the notes on Revelation 13:4. Neither his image - Revelation 13:14-15. Neither had received his mark upon their foreheads, or in their hands - Revelation 13:16. And they lived - ἔζησαν ezēsan, from ζάω zaō, "to live." Very much, in the whole passage, depends on this word 4, 5. they sat—the twelve apostles, and the saints in general. Judgment was given unto there—(Da 7:22). The office of judging was given to them. Though in one sense having to stand before the judgment-seat of Christ, yet in another sense they "do not come into judgment (Greek), but have already passed from death unto life." souls—This term is made a plea for denying the literality of the first resurrection, as if the resurrection were the spiritual one of the souls of believers in this life; the life and reign being that of the soul raised in this life from the death of sin by vivifying faith.

A Religion of Righteousness or A Martyrs Death Squad

But "souls" expresses their disembodied state (Rev 6:9) as John saw them at first; "and they lived" implies their coming to life in the body again, so as to be visible, as the phrase, Re 20:5, "this is the first resurrection," proves; for as surely as "the rest of the dead lived not (again) until," &c., refers to the bodily general resurrection, so must the first resurrection refer to the body. This also accords with 1Co 15:23, "They that are Christ's at His coming." Compare Ps 49:11-15. From Rev 6:9, I infer that "souls" is here used in the strict sense of spirits disembodied when first seen by John; though doubtless "souls" is often used in general for persons, and even for dead bodies. beheaded—literally, "smitten with an axe"; a Roman punishment, though crucifixion, casting to beasts, and burning, were the more common modes of execution. The guillotine in revolutionary France was a revival of the mode of capital punishment of pagan imperial Rome. Paul was beheaded, and no doubt shall share the first resurrection, in accordance with his prayer that he "might attain unto the resurrection from out of the rest of the dead" (Greek, "exanastasis"). The facts may account for the specification of this particular kind of punishment. For ... —Greek, "for the sake of"; on account of"; "because of "and which—Greek, "and that which." And prominent among this class (the beheaded), such as did not worship the beast. So Rev 1:7, Greek, "and which," or "and such as," particularizes prominently among the general class those that follow in the description. The extent of the first resurrection is not spoken of here. In 1Co

15:23, 51; 1Th 4:14 we find that all "in Christ" shall share in it. John himself was not "beheaded," yet who doubts but that he shall share in the first resurrection? The martyrs are put first, because most like Jesus in their sufferings and death, therefore nearest Him in their life and reign; for Christ indirectly affirms there are relative degrees and places of honor in His kingdom, the highest being for those who drink his cup of suffering. Next shall be those who have not bowed to the world power, but have looked to the things unseen and eternal.

neither—"not yet."

foreheads ... hands—Greek, "forehead ... hand."

reigned with Christ—over the earth

This is a very difficult text. Thrones are places of dignity and judicature; they seem here to signify only places of dignity. And they sat upon them; those mentioned afterward in this text sat upon them. And judgment was given unto them; that is, a power of judgment, 1 Corinthians 6:2, 3, to be executed afterward. The persons sitting upon these thrones are described to be: 1. Such as had kept themselves from idolatry, or any compliance with antichrist, either in the form of the beast, or of the image of the beast. 2. And for that non-compliance had suffered death, and for witnessing to the truths of Christ contained in his word above all else.

A Religion of Righteousness or A Martyrs Death Squad

These are described as living with Christ in honor and dignity, all that space of the church's rest and tranquility before expressed. Our learned Dr. More interprets the thrones and judgment, concerning those thrones or places of judicature, upon which the dragon's officers sat to condemn the saints of God, from whence issued the putting to death of many of the saints of God, and thinks that in this vision there is recourse to the second thunder. Now these saints are said to live and reign with Christ a thousand years; that is, say some, in heaven, in a blessed state of glory, while the militant church upon the earth enjoyed great rest and quiet on earth. Others have thought that these should be raised from the dead, and live with Christ on earth these thousand years. Which notion (if true) will solve a great phenomenon, and render it not improbable, that the number of the saints on earth will, during these thousand years, be enough to rule the world, and overbalance the number of all the wicked of the earth. Those who think thus, judge there will be two resurrections; the first, of martyrs, which shall antedate the general resurrection a thousand years: but the Scripture nowhere else mentions more than one resurrection. For my own part, I shall freely confess that I do not understand this and the two next verses, nor shall I be positive as to any sense of them: for the spiritual resurrection, as to the martyrs, it was long since passed, or else they had died in their sins. {Revelation 20:5}

And I saw thrones, and they sat upon them ... Besides the throne of God the Father, and the throne of glory, on which the Son of God sits, and the twelve thrones for the twelve apostles of the Lamb; there will be thrones set, or pitched, for all the saints, Daniel 7:9 who will sit on them, in the character of kings, and as conquerors, and shall sit quiet, and undisturbed, and be in perfect ease, and peace, for they that sit on them are the same persons hereafter described in this verse; for after the binding of Satan, an account is given of the happiness and glory of the saints during that time: and judgment was given unto them; that is, power, dominion, regal authority, possession of a kingdom, answerable to their character as kings, and to their position, sitting on thrones, Daniel 7:22 unless it should be rather understood of justice being done them, which does not so manifestly take place in the present state of things, and of which they sometimes complain; but now righteous judgment will be given for them, and against their enemies; their persons will be openly declared righteous; their characters will be cleared of all false imputations fastened on them; and their works and sufferings for Christ will be taken notice of in a way of grace, and rewarded in a very glorious manner. And so it may respect their being judged themselves, but not their judging of others, the wicked, which is the sole work of Christ; nor will the wicked now be upon the spot to be judged; nor is that notion to be supported by Matthew 19:28, 1 Corinthians 6:2, 1 Corinthians 6:3.

A Religion of Righteousness or A Martyrs Death Squad

The Jews fancy that their chief men shall judge the world in the time to come; for so they say, "in future time, (or in the world to come,) the holy blessed God will sit, and kings will place thrones for the great men of Israel, and they shall sit and judge the nations of the world with the holy blessed God:" but the persons here meant are not Jews, but sufferers for the sake of Jesus, as follows:

and I saw the souls of them that were beheaded for the witness of Jesus, and for the word of God: these, with the persons described in the next clause, are they who will sit on thrones, during the thousand years of Satan's being bound, and will have judgment given them; even such who have bore witness to the truth of Jesus being the Son of God, the true Messiah, and the only Savior of sinners, and to him as the essential Word of God, or to the written word of God, the whole Gospel, all the truths and doctrines of it; and who have been beheaded for bearing such a testimony, as John the Baptist was, the first of the witnesses of Jesus: and since this kind of punishment was a Roman one, it seems particularly to point at such persons who suffered under the Roman Pagan emperors, and to design the same souls said to be under the altar, and to cry for vengeance, Revelation 6:9. This clause, in connection with the former, is differently rendered; the Syrian version renders it thus, "and judgment was given to them, and to the souls that were beheaded" the Arabic version, "and to them was given the judgment the souls killed", the Ethiopic version, "and then I saw a seat, and the son of man sat upon it, and he rendered to them judgment for the souls of them that were slain for the law of the Lord Jesus". And which had not worshipped the beast, neither his image, neither had received his mark upon their foreheads, or in their hands, see Revelation 13:1. This describes such who shall have made no profession of the Popish religion, nor have supported it in any way; who shall not have joined in the idolatry of the Romish antichrist, but shall have protested against it, and departed from it, and shall have adhered to Christ, and to the true worship of God; see Revelation 14:1. And so this, with the preceding character, includes all the saints that lived under Rome Pagan, and Rome Papal, to the destruction of antichrist, and the setting up of Christ's kingdom; not that these martyrs and confessors, or even all the saints of their times, are the only persons that shall share in the glory and happiness of the thousand years' reign of Christ, and binding of Satan; for all the saints will come with Christ, and all the dead in Christ will rise first, or be partakers of the first resurrection; and all that are redeemed by his blood, of whatsoever nation, or in whatsoever age of the world they have lived, even from the beginning of it, shall be kings and priests, and reign with him on earth, Zechariah 14:5 though John only takes notice of these, because the design of this book, and of the visions shown to him, was only to give a prophetic history of the church, from his time, to the end of the world; and these particularly are observed to encourage the saints under sufferings for Christ:

A Religion of Righteousness or A Martyrs Death Squad

and they lived; meaning not spiritually, for so they did before, and while they bore their testimony to Christ, and against antichrist, and previous to their death; nor in their successors, for it would not be just and reasonable that they should be beheaded for their witness of Christ and his word, and others should live and reign with Christ in their room and stead; nor is this to be understood of their living in their souls, for so they live in their separate state; the soul never dies; God is not the God of the dead, but of the living: but the sense is, that they lived again, as in Revelation 20:5 they lived corporeally; their souls lived in their bodies, their bodies being raised again, and reunited to their souls, their whole persons lived; or the souls of them that were beheaded lived; that is, their bodies lived again, the soul being sometimes put for the body, Psalm 16:10 and this is called the first resurrection in the next verse: and reigned with Christ a thousand years; as all that suffer with him will, and as all that will live godly must, and do, 2 Timothy 2:12 2 Timothy 3:12. Christ being descended from heaven, and having bound Satan, and the dead saints being raised, and the living ones changed, he will reign among them personally, visibly, and gloriously, and in the fullest manner; all the antichristian powers will be destroyed; Satan will be in close confinement; death, with respect to Christ and his people, will be no more; the heavens and the earth will be made new, and all things will be subject to him; and all his saints will be with him, and they shall reign with him; they shall be glorified together; they shall sit on the throne with him, have a crown of righteousness given them, and possess the kingdom appointed for them; they will reign over all their enemies; Satan will be bruised under their feet, being bound; the wicked will be shut up in hell, and neither will be able to give them any disturbance; and sin and death will be no more: this reign will not be in a sensual and carnal way, or lie in possessing worldly riches and honors, in eating and drinking, marrying, and giving in marriage; the saints will not be in a mortal, but in an immortal state; the children of this resurrection will be like the angels; and this reign will be on earth, Revelation 5:10 the present earth will be burnt up, and a new one formed, in which these righteous persons will dwell, 2 Peter 3:13 of which See Gill on Revelation 21:1 and it will last a thousand years; not distinct from, but the same with the thousand years in which Satan will be bound; for if they were distinct from them, and should commence when they are ended, the reign of Christ with his saints would be when Satan is loosed, which is utterly inconsistent with it. The Syriac version very rightly renders it, these thousand years, referring to those of Satan's binding. Nor are these thousand years to be understood prophetically, for as many years as there are days in a thousand years; for as this would defer the judgment of the wicked, and the ultimate glory of the saints, to a prodigious length of time, so it should be observed, that prophetic time will now be no longer, according to the angel's oath in Revelation 10:6 but these are to be understood literally and definitely, as before, of just such an exact number and term of years; 2 Peter 3:8 this is a perfect number, and is expressive of the perfection of this state, and is a term of years that neither Adam, nor any of his sons, arrived unto; but Christ the second Adam shall see his seed, and shall prolong his days longer than any of them, Isaiah 53:10. It is an observation of the Jewish Rabbins that the day in Genesis 2:17 is the day of the holy blessed God (a thousand years), and therefore the first Adam did not perfect or fill up his day for there wanted seventy years of it and it is a notion that prevails with them, that the days of the Messiah will be a thousand years and so they will be at his second coming, but not at his first which they vainly expect it being past: and also they say that in these thousand years God will renew his world, and that then the righteous will be raised, and no more return to dust; which agrees with John's new heaven and new earth during this state, and with the first resurrection: and so the Rabbins, says that the Jews expect a thousand years' reign.

The Geneva Study Bible

{6} And I saw {a} thrones, and they sat upon them, and {7} judgment was given unto them: and *I saw* the souls of them that were {8} beheaded for the witness of Jesus, and for the word of God, and which {9} had not worshipped the beast, neither his image, neither had received *his* mark upon their foreheads, or in their hands; and they lived and reigned with Christ a thousand years. (6) A description of the common state of the Church of Christ in earth in that space of a thousand years, during which the devil was in bonds; in which first the authority, life, and common honor of the godly,

(6) A description of the common state of the Church of Christ in earth in that space of a thousand years, during which the devil was in bonds; in which first the authority, life, and common honor of the godly, is declared, Rev 20:4. Secondly, newness of life is preached to others by the gospel after that time; Rev 20:5. Finally, he concludes with promises, Rev 20:6. (a) For judgment was committed to them, as to members joined to the head: not that Christ's office was given over to them. (7) This was a type of the authority of the good and faithful servants of God in the Church, taken from the manner of men. (8) Of the martyrs, who suffered in those first times?

(9) Of the martyrs who suffered after both the beasts were now risen up, chapter 15. For there, these things are expounded.

4. thrones] Daniel 7:9, "They" who sat upon them, to whom judgment (the right of judging: 1 Corinthians 6:2-3) was given are identified by Daniel 7:22 as "the saints of the Most High"—saints, plainly, in the modern sense, as distinguished from angels. [I saw] the souls] Revelation 6:9. beheaded] Lit, Struck with the axe, the old Roman mode of execution by sentence of the supreme magistrate. Capital punishment of citizens had been virtually abolished for the last years of the Republic: and when the emperors assumed the right of executing men for treason, it was done as though by military law (Mark 6:27), by a soldier with a sword. But the old constitutional punishment was inflicted on provincials down to the fall of the Republic and it is not impossible that it was revived

when it was desired that a citizen should be executed in due form of law. Thus it is not unlikely that St Paul will be included among those thus designated. which had not worshipped] Revelation 13:12; Revelation 13:15-16, reigned with Christ] 2 Timothy 2:12. This "reign" was foretold in Revelation 5:10. "The nations" of the world continue to exist as usual (Revelation 5:3), so it is no doubt over them that the saints and martyrs reign. A thousand years] Only in this passage is the kingdom of Christ on earth (which is of course one of the most frequent subjects of prophecy) designated as a millennium or period of 1000 years. It may be added, that this is the only prophecy where there is at all good reason for supposing that the Millennium of popular belief is indicated, as distinct on the one hand from the Kingdom of God which already exists in the Christian Church, and on the other from that which will be set up at the last day. Nevertheless, this passage is quite sufficient foundation for the doctrine, even if it stood alone: and there are many other prophecies which, if not teaching it so plainly, may fairly be understood to refer to it, if the doctrine be admitted to be according to the mind of the Spirit. We therefore have to consider the question, Is this prophecy to be understood literally? Is it meant that, for a period of a thousand years (or more), before the general Resurrection and the end of this world, this earth will be the scene of a blessed visible Kingdom of God, wherein the power of the Devil will have vanished, and that of Christ be supreme and unopposed?

Wherein Christ shall either reign visibly on earth, or at least shall make His presence felt far more unmistakably than at present; while the martyrs and other great saints of all past time shall rise, and, whether on earth or in heaven, share in the glory of His reign? Down to the fourth century, the decidedly dominant belief of Christendom was in favor of this literal interpretation of the prophecy: since then, at least till the Reformation, it has been still more decidedly against it. In the second century, Papias, who seems to have been more or less personally acquainted with St John himself, taught Millenarian doctrine decidedly: and St Irenaeus and others derived it from him. In the same age St Justin accepted the doctrine, though admitting that Christians were not unanimous on the subject: but he considers St John's authority, in this passage, decisive. And in fact, the rejection of the doctrine was usually on the part of those who rejected or questioned the authority of the Revelation as a whole: it was held to discredit the book, that it taught the doctrine. Thus in the third century, Caius the Roman Presbyter seems unmistakably to ascribe the book, not to St John but to his adversary Cerinthus; on the ground of its teaching this carnal and Jewish doctrine of an earthly kingdom of Christ. And St Dionysius of Alexandria, who, though not admitting the book to be the work of St John the Apostle, yet on the whole recognizes its inspiration and authority, thinks it necessary to refute a suffragan (asst. bishop of his own, who adopted Millenarian views, as though he were at least on the verge of heresy. The case seems to have stood thus. The doctrine of the Millennium was current in the Church, but was most insisted on in that section of the Church whose Jewish affinities were strongest: and it is asserted—it is very likely true—that the heretical Judaizers expressed their millennial hopes in a coarse and carnal form. Orthodox Christians condemned their language: but while some of them, like Justin, felt bound, in obedience to the plain teaching of St John, to believe in a Millennium of spiritual blessedness on earth, others, like Caius, rejected altogether the doctrine of the Millennium, and rejected, if necessary, the Apocalypse as teaching it. But when St Dionysius proposed to reject millennial doctrine without rejecting the authority of the Apocalypse, a course was suggested which, if less critically and logically defensible, was theologically safer than either. The Apocalypse was declared not really to foretell a millennium, but only such a kingdom of Christ as all prophecy does foretell, a Church such as now exists. To expect His more perfect kingdom to be an earthly and temporal one was pronounced a heresy, a falling back to Judaism. St Jerome who, living in Palestine, knew more than most men of the Judaizing heresies which still existed in his time, and had once been formidable, spoke very strongly (as his manner was) in condemnation of the Milliarii (this, not Millenarii, is the ancient Latin name of the sect). He apparently grouped together all believers in the earthly kingdom, whether they regarded its delights as carnal or not: and it seems that his strong language frightened the Church of his time into giving it up. St Augustine had held and taught the doctrine, of course in a pure and spiritual form: but towards the close of his life he abandoned it, and though admitting his old belief to be tolerable, he echoes Jerome's condemnation of the Judaizing caricature of it. The opinion of these two great Fathers was adopted by the Church down to the Reformation, not formally or synodically, but as a matter of popular tradition. At the Reformation, the Anabaptists proclaimed an earthly kingdom of Christ in the Millenarian sense, and certainly did all they could to discredit the doctrine, by the carnal form in which they held it. There was a tendency to revive the doctrine, among sober Protestants: but the alarm raised by the Anabaptists at first went far to counteract it; e.g. in England one of the 42 Articles of 1552 condemned it as "Jewish dotage." But when the controversies of the Reformation quieted down, and both the Romanist and the Protestant Churches formulated their own beliefs, the former adhered to the tradition of SS. Jerome and Augustine, while the latter, for the most part, as was natural, went back to the literal sense of Scripture and the older tradition. It thus appears that Catholic consent cannot fairly be alleged either for or against the literal interpretation. Catholic feeling does of course condemn a Judaizing or carnal view of the nature of Christ's Kingdom: but whether He will have a kingdom on earth more perfect, or reign more visibly, than is the case now, is a point on which Christians may lawfully differ; the Church has not pronounced either way. If the question be theologically open, it appears that, as a matter of opinion, the literal sense is to be preferred: "when the literal sense will stand, that furthest from the letter is the worst." Can anyone honestly say, that Satan has been bound during the time (already far more than a thousand years) that the kingdom of Christ on earth has already existed?

A Religion of Righteousness or A Martyrs Death Squad

That he deceives the nations no more till the present dispensation approaches its end in the days of Antichrist? It is far easier to hold that he will be bound for a long time (probably more rather than less than a thousand literal years), after Antichrist has been overthrown, but before the actual end of the world. Revelation 20:4. An axe, especially used by the Romans in punishments, Raphelius compares the passage of Polybius lived, returned to life, [in that manner, in which the rest of the dead lived not again before the general resurrection.—The same word is thus used with the same force in Revelation 20:5 and Revelation 2:8. John saw them not only when restored to life, but when in the act of reviving (comp. Ezekiel 37:7): as before he saw the dragon in the act of being bound, and not only in that condition with, they shall be with Christ (Revelation 20:6), and with God (Revelation 20:6), not Christ and God with them. Therefore that kingdom will be in heaven. Comp. Revelation 21:3, with a thousand years) They who are held back by the article here improperly inserted before greatly entangle themselves. Two millennial periods are mentioned in this whole passage, each three times: the former is the millennium in which Satan is bound, Revelation 20:2-3; Revelation 20:7; the other, that of the reign of the saints, Revelation 20:4-6. A theologian finds no foundation for two periods of a thousand years, either in the text, or in the event itself, or in the connection of the parts of the Apocalypse. But the second millennium extends even to the resurrection of all the dead, Revelation 20:5; the former comes to a close before the end of the world, Revelation 20:7.

Therefore the beginning and end of the former is before the beginning and end of the second. On this account, as at Revelation 20:2 in the first mention of the former millennium, so at Revelation 20:4, in the first mention of the second, it is said without the article, in the other places, the article having the force of a relative, and meaning those thousand years, Revelation 20:3; Revelation 20:5; Revelation 20:7. Finally, without the article, is used in Revelation 20:6, as though in a separate enunciation. The omission of the article conveys a less restricted meaning than its insertion. Many admit, that the millennium in which Satan is bound, is different from the millennium in which the saint's reign, this distinction between the two periods of a thousand years affords a great advantage, and that too of such necessity, as to prove this very distinctness of the millennial periods. In the judgment of an illustrious man, a serious difficulty is raised by the hope of better times, or even by the reconciling of the millennial kingdom itself with the final perverseness and damnable security of men of the last times. The keeping the times distinct alone remedies this difficulty. During the course of the former millennium, the promises which describe most flourishing times of the Church will be fulfilled: Revelation 10:7; afterwards, while the saints who belong to the first resurrection shall reign with Christ, men on earth will be remiss and careless, Matthew 24:37, etc.; according to which explanation that remarkable passage, Luke 18:8, retains the natural meaning of the words. Respecting this [false] security, which will seize men, when the enemies are now removed, there is a valuable suggestion subjoined to the commentary of

A Religion of Righteousness or A Martyrs Death Squad

Patrick Forbes on the Apocalypse confounding of the two millennial periods has long ago produced many errors, and has made the name of Chiliasm hateful and suspected; the distinction between the two resolves the difficulties to which Chiliasm is justly liable, and aids in the sound interpretation of prophecy. As to what remains, what can orthodoxy itself blame? Let them pronounce sentence, on whose authority others depend. Add, that they who neither extend the remaining times of the world beyond the truth of Scripture, nor curtail them, they alone are well able to meet and contend with scoffers. This is the last period in the age of the world; wherefore in this place we will comprehensively repeat an analysis of the times, which we have already abundantly spoken of, with sobriety and modesty. The same age of the world comprises 7777 7/9 natural years, which are 490 prophetical months. Therefore a perfect septenary is displayed, I will not here say in the natural days, and that indeed a square, but in the prophetical months, and that indeed a square; in the natural years, it is seen through all the expressed articles of the whole sum, from the thousandth to the unit, and below. This TESSELATED CONFORMATION of times, natural and prophetical, of those of Daniel and those of the Apocalypse, ought to convince of their truth everyone who has any capacity for receiving this kind of truth.

This describes the position of Christians in this life. They sit upon thrones; that is, they reign with Christ. Judgment is given unto them; that is, by their conduct in the world the world is judged and condemned. St. John continually thus describes the Christian's position; and such a picture is especially applicable for his purpose here, which is to portray the glory of the Christian calling, and the certainty of the Christian's hope. The redeemed have been made kings, and reign (Revelation 5:10). So also St. Paul says we are "blessed with all spiritual blessings in heavenly places in Christ" (Ephesians 1:2). And I saw the souls of them that were beheaded for the witness of Jesus, and for the Word of God, and which had not worshipped the beast, neither his image, neither had received his mark upon their foreheads, or in their hands. This is a special reference to the martyrs made with the object mentioned above that of encouraging Christians in their warfare. The class here described forms part of the whole body of Christians alluded to in the first part of the verse (Revelation 6:10; Revelation 1:9; Revelation 12:17; Revelation 19:10; also Revelation 13; Revelation 15:2). In the same way the souls referred to in Revelation 6:9 are those existing during the period of this world, which we have here understood to be denoted indirectly by the "thousand years." And they lived and reigned with Christ a thousand years. "The thousand years" adopted in the Textus Receptus, is found in others, but omitted. "They lived and reigned with Christ" in complete and perfect assurance, as in ver. 2, and for the reason given in ver. 2, that, Satan was bound completely.

A Religion of Righteousness or A Martyrs Death Squad

This living and reigning must not be limited to the period after the death of the martyrs (though it is doubtless true in this sense also), notwithstanding the fact that St. John sees them here after their death. It is as though he would say, "You Christians sit upon thrones and reign with Christ; yea, even those who suffered shameful deaths shared this perfect safety and exaltation, though to the eyes of the world they were so afflicted and degraded." They lived is described in ver. 5 as the "first resurrection." This can only be referred to that first awakening from sin to the glorious life of the gospel, which St. John elsewhere describes in a similar manner. "He that hears my Word... has everlasting life, and shall not come into condemnation; but is passed from death unto life" (John 5:24); "We have passed from death unto life" (1 John 3:14).

Part II:

A

Martyrs

Death Squad

CHAPTER IV

The Spirit of the Antichrist

ANTICHRIST AND THE SPIRIT OF ANTICHRIST

The Coming World Leader has over 30 titles in the Old Testament and 13 in the New Testament. One of the most identifying titles is The Prince That Shall Come, from Daniel 9:26-27 which connects his origin with those who destroyed the temple, which makes him a Roman and a gentile. He is commonly known as the Antichrist, But What is Antichrist? 1 John 2:22-23 "Who is the liar but the one who denies that Jesus is the Christ? <u>He is antichrist</u>, who denies the Father and the Son. Whoever denies the Son does not have the Father; the one who acknowledges the Son has the Father also." This is someone who denies Christ as the only anointed one and refuses the interrelationship of the persons who are deity. 1 John 4:2-3 "By this you know the Spirit of God: every spirit that confesses that Jesus Christ has come in the flesh is from God; and every spirit that does not confess Jesus is not from God; and this is <u>the spirit of the antichrist</u>, of which you have heard that it is coming, and now it is already in the world."

Several times this term is used in the plural, and can be applied to almost anyone who is opposed to Christ. Those who deny that Jesus came in the flesh are anti-Christ or of the spirit of antichrist. This is one of the ways to discern a false teacher from a true one. John is writing after the resurrection and is using *perfect tense* in Greek which denotes a past action with continuing results into the present, and continuing on into the future. He came in the flesh, rose in the flesh, and is still in the flesh.

The same body that He was born and died with, He rose with. If one claims that Christ rose as a spirit creature and not physically they are of the Anti - Christ spirit and are denying the third point of the Gospel. It was the Gnostics that John is specifically addressing in his epistles. The word Anti can be understood to mean either against Christ or it can also means in place of, a substitute is the fuller meaning. He will be a substitute for the real one. In this way he opposes him. The common use of this title applies to the great world dictator, the last Caesar in the end times. He is Satan's chosen vehicle the beast receiving from the dragon dominion and power (Rev.13:2).

SPIRIT of Anti Christ

Right now people are being conditioned as never before to accept the great lie....the DELUSION that will bring his leadership upon everyone who rejects the gospel. The new age influence is found in the Movies and through the TV and popular books conditioning people to believe in other type beings out there, that we are not alone in the universe. The 'Hollywood' promotion of X files, Independence day, Dark Skies, Earth's final conflict is not too favorable. However Close Encounters, ET, Contact, Alf and numerous other films and TV show our openness to other life forms. Star Treks Babylon five series with a united federation of planets with all kinds of alien races in the universe living together in peace and harmony.

Von Daniken's book *Chariot of the Gods* has been accepted as an alternative to our ancient past. Myths are promoted in books and TV that we are star seeds of another race that is coming back to visit us. This is the new age fable of a spiritual hierarchy of ascended masters which are spirit guides sent to govern the human race through history. These views are a logical as well as entertaining alternative to those who refuse the truth of creationism and have already embraced in the lie of evolution. After the rapture when the restraint is removed the demons who are the fallen angels already disguised as 'aliens' spirit guides and ascended maters, will come forward and offer their peace plan to the world. This will eventually become a contract between Israel and the prince that will come Dan.9:24-26. This will be a time of spiritual revival called "mystery Babylon" with All kinds of signs, wonders, and lying miracles which will be exhibited to the world by spirit beings called masters that will work through their servants of deception. Since the world has rejected the Lord Jesus, the true Christ, they will accept the devil's substitute with open arms. He will look good as it gets, since he will embrace all and reject only one, Christ and his followers who claim there is only one way.

Types of Anti Christ

The bible teaches there are many antichrists and we can find types that exhibit his nature somewhere in the different men of history.

Nebuchadnezzar was a type of antichrist having an image made of gold and people were to bow down to it. Its correlation 2 Thess.2.. Haman in the book of Esther was a type of the Antichrist making a law for the Jews bow down to the king with intentions of wiping them out. Pharaoh was a type of an antichrist worshipped as God who enslaved the Jews. Pharaoh and his army came after the children of Israel like Satan does in Rev.12. Nero was a type of the antichrist asking people to bow down to him adding himself to their worship, killing Christians who refused. Many powerful rulers have acted this way on the stage of human history. Genghis Khan, Stalin, Hitler are only a few men that bring memories of horror in their rule of enslavement.

Many powerful rulers have acted this way on the stage of human history. Genghis Khan, Stalin, Hitler are only a few men that bring memories of horror in their rule of enslavement. But there is one who at the end of time unites and rules the entire world and all religions. He is called the man of sin, the son of perdition who will make them all look like kindergartners. Rev. 13:13: "He <u>performs great signs,</u> so that he even makes fire come down from heaven on the earth in the sight of men.:14 And he deceives those who dwell on the earth <u>by those signs</u> which he was granted to do in the sight of the beast, telling those who dwell on the earth to make an image <u>to the beast who was wounded by the sword and lived.</u>" This is fake resurrection that will bring awe to those on our planet.

Rev 16:14: "For they are spirits of demons, performing signs, which go out to the kings of the earth and of the whole world, to gather them to the battle of that great day of God Almighty." His army of spirit beings will deceive the governments so that they will want to do battle against Christ when he comes back. He is the one who will be totally energized by Satan and will be able to do miracles (2 Thess2: 9) for the purpose of world-wide deception. He is the one who will be totally energized by Satan and will be able to do miracles (2 Thess2: 9) for the purpose of world-wide deception,

Judas son of Perdition

Do we see this spirit work today! The antichrist prefigured by Judas is not a Hitler. He does not fit the outline of most interpretations of the antichrist. Judas was a professing member of the church, and he was respected by the other disciples. He was entrusted with the treasury he went out with them and appears to have cast out demons and heal. Unfortunately he was unsuccessful to do this on himself. The Bible calls Judas "the son of perdition." Judas is a type of Antichrist in that he illustrates some of his characteristics. (John 17:12 This expression is used in only one other passage in Scripture, 2 Thessalonians 2:3.)There it applies to Antichrist standing in the holy place sits in temple showing himself to be God. How? By lying signs and wonders he deceives those who are lost. To the elect his purpose is to remove them from the faith and be a substitute for the person of Christ.

The Descendants of Ishmael

This is why spiritual power is not a credential of being from God; Satan can perform his own powerful works, either through deception or through his own spiritual resources as 2 Thess. 2:9 states "The coming of the lawless one is according to the working of Satan, with <u>all power</u>, signs, and lying wonders," We call Judas a betrayer, but that is not how he viewed himself. He thought he would speed up the eventual and probably make some money to boot. After all following Jesus he should have money and nice things as he rules over the people. Judas professed to follow Christ. He walked and ate with him. On the fateful night he kisses Jesus in his betrayal selling him for 30 pieces. That is Antichrist. Judas still thought he was a disciple when he did this. Maybe he thought that Jesus would work a miracle when the soldiers came for him. He wanted the Messiah to cast off the Roman yoke through a major display of miracle power and be crowned king, he wanted the kingdom now. Judas thought he was helping Jesus obtain what was rightfully His. Take the kingdom by force, not the meek will inherit the earth. But this was not the way Jesus intended it. Paul Henri Spaak of Belgium, one of the organizational leaders of the Society for Worldwide Interbank Financial Telecommunication said to the United European Community: "What we want is a man of sufficient stature to hold the allegiance of all people, to lift us out of the economic morass into which we are sinking. Send us such a man, and whether he be <u>god or devil</u>, we will receive him." So the world leaders are open for whoever can come along to solve the political dilemma and make peace.

The Spirit of the Antichrist

They are desperate they will take anyone even the Devil who will claim to be god. Another biblical type of the Antichrist is given in the person of Antiochus Epiphanes, a Gentile. He went in and desolated the temple. Nowhere is a Gentile seen as a type of Christ; and with good reason, for Christ Himself was to be a Jew. So here, the type of the Antichrist is a Gentile, Antiochus Epiphanies. The reason is that the Antichrist himself is to be a Gentile. Another argument for the Gentile nature of the Antichrist is found *in biblical imagery.* Whenever the word "sea" is used symbolically in the Scriptures, especially in the book of the Revelation, it is a symbol of the Gentile nations. Since the first Beast in Revelation 13:1-10 arises out of the sea, and the sea represents the Gentile world or nations (Revelation 17:15), the Antichrist is of Gentile origin. His title summarizes his nature. He will be *anti*, "opposed to," Christ in every area of character and conduct. This means also to his Jewishness, he will be a gentile messiah, he will be anti-Jewish. Look at some of the similarities. Christ came from above. John. 6:38 "For I have come down from heaven." The Antichrist the beast comes from the pit. Rev. 11:7 The beast that comes out of the abyss. From the Sea Rev.13:1 from the earth Rev.13:11. Not from heaven, from God but earthly, demonic. Christ humbled himself. Phil. 2:8 "And being found in appearance as a man, He humbled himself." Antichrist exalts himself. 2 Thess. 2:4 "Who opposes and exalts himself above every so called god." Self exaltation, Christ came in his father's name. John 5:43: "I have come in my Father's name and you do not receive me."

Antichrist comes in his own name. John 5:43 "Another shall come in his own name you will receive him." self proclamation. Christ came to do His Fathers will. John 6:38: "For I have come down from Heaven not to do my own will, but the will of Him that sent me." Antichrist comes to do his own will. Dan.11:38 "Then the king will do as he pleases, and he will exalt and magnify himself above every god." Self willed. Christ is the Holy one. Lk.4:34 I know who you are the- Holy one of God." Antichrist is known as the Lawless one. 2 Thess.2:8"and then the Lawless one will be revealed." He hides his identity, but Christ reveals it. Christ is the Son of God having the same nature as his Father Luke 1:35 "That Holy one that is to be born will be called the Son of God." The Antichrist is the son of Perdition having the same nature as Satan. 2 Thess. 2:3 "And that man of sin be revealed the son of perdition." Many other parallels could be cited to show that he comes to copy in the very opposite what Christ did. But this will not be so obvious at first because it will be deceptive; he will be substitute an Anti-Christ. 2 Thess. 2 tells us he will have all power, not only politically but supernaturally to perform <u>all signs and lying wonders</u>. These miracles lie because the source is not from God but they can look just like something from God. They will be so powerful and deceptive the only way one will be able to discern is from knowing the word to apply a test to them. Scripture tells us how to identify the man of sin He will come disguised as an angel of light. He will come to the world as a man of peace at first. He will be given supernatural strength to show signs and perform wonders.

He will exalt himself and magnify himself above every god. He also will have the number 666 that is the value of his name. He will corrupt men and gain their allegiance through deceit and flattery. Rev 13:3-15 *"He performs great signs*, so that he even makes fire come down from heaven on the earth in the sight of men.(fire and light in the O.T and new are related to the glory of God in the temple, at Elijah's altar, at the transfiguration and at Pentecost, so he will counterfeit this)14 And he deceives those who dwell on the earth by those signs which he was granted to do in the sight of the beast, *telling those who dwell on the earth to make an image to the beast who was wounded by the sword and lived.* (To my knowledge no Pope has done any signs and wonders yet. Jesus said this would be his basis of operation Mt.24:24. Notice it states the whole earth makes an image of the beast, where would this be? 2 Thess, Again tells us it will be erected in the temple. 15 He was granted power to give breath to the image of the beast, that the image of the beast should both speak <u>and cause as many as would not worship the image of the beast to be killed</u>." (This beast will be a miracle worker like no one else, he has the power to give life to this image and it speaks, he also kills those who are not worshipping the image. Is the image a day as some claim? Unless you spiritualize this passage, it is a look alike of the beast. Consider all the miracles that have to do with statues today inside and outside the Catholic Church, we can see it already operating. Statues of the Virgin Mary and Jesus are reported to `cry' tears of human blood or olive oil, counseling observers to return to the spiritual path. (numerous sources) Rocking Madonna of

The Descendants of Ishmael

Ballinspittle, Ireland the statue moves back and forth as you view it from the bottom of a small hill. But this is not the only place miracles like this are occurring, they are happening all over the world in different religions. Greenville Sun, Virginian Pilot, Pasadena Star-News, Manila Bulletin, and others report Radiant crosses of light, are seen by tens of thousands from California to the Philippines, it brings spontaneous healings . Rainbow colored light emanates from an image of Maitreya Buddha which suddenly appeared on a bathroom window of a home in Nagano City, Japan. In Senegal and the UK, Muslim families discover the symbol for Allah formed on or in garden of vegetables. Reuters reported A 12-year-old Lebanese girl produces tiny crystals from her eyes. In Nairobi, Kenya, a man appears `out of the blue' He appeared miraculously before 6,000 people at a prayer meeting. Many in attendance are healed. He then leaves in an equally mysterious manner, promising to return with a "bucketful of blessings". He was photographed addressing (in their own language) thousands of people who instantly recognized Him as the Christ. The story and photo were carried by news media around the world. (Kenya Times, BBC, CNN and newspapers worldwide) worshippers at Muslim Village, Kawangware, Nairobi, believe they saw Jesus Christ, in broad daylight. "Whole villages are visited by the "man in white robes"; people see him and recognize him.

The Spirit of the Antichrist

They call him Aisa, the Muslim Arabic name for Jesus." The man in white is now known to many." (Source: Evangelical Broadcasting Company, Holland) It is Maitreya who calls himself Christ. His recent appearances are in Thessalonica Afghanistan and Bolivia. Since late 1991 Maitreya has been carrying out a series of appearances like the one in Nairobi, Kenya... Dutch television viewers watching a program entitled Healing and Faith, made by the Evangelical Broadcasting company, recently heard eyewitness accounts of miraculous healings and of many places in the Middle East where "the man in white" is known A continuous wave of miraculous phenomena including crosses of light, manifestations of Jesus and Mary in the clouds, weeping statues of the Madonna, milk-drinking Hindu icons, wells of healing water in Mexico, Germany and elsewhere, are occurring with more & more frequency. His restraining seems to be slowly removed until at once it will no longer restrain. Benjamin Crème the harbinger for the new age Christ states "the world today is filled with miracles ... Maitreya says those who search for signs will find them (this is the very reason Jesus said not to do so, a warning to those being trained in the church to look for the signs). "But the world is filled with signs of his presence ... the appearances of the Modanna all over the world, the moving Modanna the statues ... (Just like the life that will be given to the image of the beast in the temple that is soon to be built). "The icons of Jesus which cry, the Madonna's which cry real tears sometimes blood this is happening by the hundreds and thousands all over the world.

The Descendants of Ishmael

Now in the eastern world among the Hindus we have the extraordinary milk miracle in September 1996 when for 4 days the statues of kanesha and Shivah would often lap up the milk the milk virtually disappeared by the millions of gallons the milk ran dry in India... (*Hinduism Today* and numerous other newspapers worldwide) (Benjamen Creme on an Art Bell program talked about TV cameras filming a statue drinking milk. Even the camera operators would hold out the milk in a cap or a spoon to the statue which is made of wood and the milk literally disappeared. That I think is the most widespread and great types of miracle which has happened in the world. ..." The milk was of course not drunk by the statue made of brass... it was made to disappear by Maitreya and a group of masters who do that type of thing (like James and Jambres deception, a good supernatural parlor trick by spirits.) However, the deception can only take root in those who do not receive the love of the truth; they want a lie, and God will send them a strong delusion. 2 Thess. 2:10 and 11, that those who reject the gospel now will not be given a second chance after the Rapture, God will send them a strong delusion that they should not be saved. The people who make the eternal mistake of receiving the mark and worshiping the beast and/or his image will be deceived by accompanying miraculous signs and wonders which they think takes place from the real Christ: All the miracles we see today have to do with Idolatry. Apparitions, statues moving eyes, crying, blood, and milk drank by a statue .This is all specifically addressed in Rev.13:14 and 2 Thess.2:2 as a warning.

As the evil generation went after Jesus signs when he was here in the flesh it appears it will be the same for that last generation. The Bible tells us that in the last days one man will rule the world. He will rule over the entire human race politically, economically and religiously speaking great blasphemies against God and setting himself up in the Temple as God himself. But this man will not be God. He will be the very antithesis. He will even <u>lead a rebellion against God</u>, but he will be destroyed by the King of kings. History has deemed him the Antichrist, but he is known by other names as well, each being fully indicative of his character:

The Little Horn - **Daniel 7:8** (TKESB) The Fierce King, a Master of Intrigue - **Daniel 8:23** (TKESB) The Prince Who is to Come - **Daniel 9:26** (TKESB) The Worthless Shepherd - **Zechariah 11:17** (TKESB)The Man of Lawlessness–. . . . . **2 Thessalonians 2:3** (TKESB) The One Who Brings Destruction - **2 Thessalonians 2:3** (TKESB) The Beast - **Revelation 13:11** (TKESB) Through careful study of the Scriptures, we can learn much about the origins, disposition, and career of the one human being who will be the literal embodiment of Satan himself.

His Nationality

The Bible provides us with some detail regarding the nationalistic origins of the Antichrist. Although much debate surrounds his national identity, the Book of Daniel clearly states that he will come from the people whose armies destroy the Temple.

The Descendants of Ishmael

"A ruler will arise whose armies will destroy the city and the Temple." **Daniel 9:26** The City and the Temple were destroyed in A.D. 70 by Titus and the Roman legions, but Titus was not the ruler referenced in this verse. For Daniel 9:27 describes the ruler as one who will make a seven-year treaty with Israel, put an end to the sacrifices and offerings, and set up a sacrilegious object that causes desecration. These are events that will be fulfilled in the life of the Antichrist. According to Daniel, the Antichrist will come from among the people who destroyed the Temple. Therefore, we can be certain the Antichrist is of Roman descent. However, being of Roman descent does not automatically mean that the Antichrist will be Italian. It simply means he must come from among those people who were part of the Roman Empire of that time. Daniel Chapter 8 provides us with further insight. In it, the angel Gabriel explains Daniel's vision of a Ram and Goat as events relating to the Greek Empire of Alexander the Great. In a claim verified by history, he states that following the death of Alexander, the empire will be divided into four parts. From one of those four parts, the Antichrist will arise: "The shaggy male goat represents the king of the Greek Empire. The four prominent horns that replaced the one large horn show that the Greek Empire will break into four sections with four kings, none of them as great as the first. At the end of their rule, when their sin is at its height, a fierce king, a master of intrigue, will rise to power. He will become very strong, but not by his own power. He will cause a shocking amount of destruction and succeed in everything he does.

He will destroy powerful leaders and devastate the holy people." **Daniel 8:21-24** Daniel Chapter 11 provides an in-depth examination of the history of the breakup Alexander's empire, describing historical events relating to the King of the North and the King of the South. The latter part of the chapter describes the Antichrist, identifying him with other historical figures that have held the title "King of the North." This, along with the passage cited above, clearly links the Antichrist to the Northern Kingdom of the divided Greek Empire. This kingdom was ruled by one of Alexander's generals, Seleucus, who ruled the areas of Syria, Mesopotamia, and Persia. Therefore, it is reasonable to assume the Antichrist will also be linked to these geographic areas.

Is the Antichrist Jewish?

Although there is no definitive answer, two Bible verses provide us with reason to believe that he will be. The first appears in the Book of Genesis when God prophesies the coming of Israel's Messiah and Satan's Antichrist. "From now on, you and the woman will be enemies, and your offspring and her offspring will be enemies. He will crush your head, and you will strike his heel." **Genesis 3:15.** Later on, when Jacob is blessing his sons, he makes this prophecy about Dan: "Dan will govern his people like any other tribe in Israel. He will be a snake beside the road, a poisonous viper along the path that bites the horse's heels so the rider is thrown off." **Genesis 49:16-17**

This reference to a serpent striking a heel may indicate that the Antichrist will be a Jew from the tribe of Dan, but many reasonable people are divided on this issue. So how do we rectify these seemingly contradictory prophecies concerning the Antichrist's nationality? Is he Roman? Italian? Jewish? Assyrian? Greek? He doesn't necessarily have to be exclusively one or another. He could be an Assyrian Jew born and raised in Italy, or any number of possible combinations. We don't know for certain, but history indicates that each of these prophecies will be harmonized when the Antichrist appear. Two thousand years ago, the seemingly contradictory <u>prophecies of the first coming of the Messiah</u> were all harmonized in the life of Jesus Christ who was a Nazarene born in Bethlehem who came out of Egypt. With the benefit of hindsight, we can see how this was possible, but for the Jewish scholars who lived before the time of Jesus, these prophecies were the topic of much debate. That debate continues today in regard to prophecies of the Antichrist. But in reality, we won't know the absolute truth until he appears. As such, it is wise to study these prophecies and teach them to others, so that the people of the Antichrist's generation will be able to positively identify him based on sound Scriptural evidence.

His Personality

Throughout the Bible, we are granted insight into the personality and disposition of the Antichrist. We are told how he will act, what he will do, and where he will get his power. Although far from exhaustive, the Scriptures provide us with many clues...

The Spirit of the Antichrist

Homosexuality

The Antichrist will be homosexual:

The Tyranny of the Western King:

Dan; 11:36-38,....The king shall do according to his will; and he shall exalt himself, and magnify himself above every god, and shall speak marvelous things against the God of gods; and he shall prosper until the indignation be accomplished for that which is determined shall be done. Neither shall he regard the gods of his fathers, nor the desire of women, nor regard any god; for he shall magnify himself above all. But in his place shall he honor the god of fortresses; and a god whom his father's didn't know shall he honor with gold, and silver, and with precious stones, and pleasant things. He shall deal with the strongest fortresses by the help of a foreign god: whoever acknowledges [him] he will increase with glory; and he shall cause them to rule over many, and shall divide the land for a price.

Habakkuk 2:4;5,...Behold, his soul is puffed up. It is not upright in him, but the righteous will live by his faith. Yes, moreover, wine is treacherous. A haughty man who doesn't stay at home, who enlarges his desire as Sheol, and he is like death, and can't be satisfied, but gathers to himself all nations, and heaps to himself all peoples.....2:15; 16 "Woe to him who gives his neighbor drink, pouring your inflaming wine until they are drunk, so that you may gaze at their naked bodies! You are filled with shame, and not glory.

You will also drink, and be exposed! The cup of God's right hand will come around to you, and disgrace will cover your glory.

Arrogance

The Antichrist will be arrogant:

"This little horn had eyes like human eyes and a mouth that was boasting arrogantly." **Daniel 7:8**

The Antichrist will be so filled with self-love and arrogance that he will launch a rebellion against God Almighty. He will place himself above all others, and even set himself up in the Jewish Temple, proclaiming himself to be God.

Satan's Power

The Antichrist will be empowered by Satan:

"He will become very strong, but not by his own power." **Daniel 8:24**

"This evil man will come to do the work of Satan with counterfeit power and signs and miracles. He will use every kind of wicked deception to fool those who are on their way to destruction because they refuse to believe the truth that would save them." **2 Thessalonians 2:9-10**

The Spirit of the Antichrist

"And the dragon gave him his own power and throne and great authority." **Revelation 13:2**

The Bible clearly states that the Antichrist will derive his power from Satan. In fact, following the Devil's banishment from heaven (Revelation 12:9), he will indwell the Antichrist, making this man of lawlessness the literal embodiment of Satan.

Beholden to Power

The Antichrist will be consumed with power and power alone will he worship:

"He will have no regard for the god of his ancestors, or for the god beloved of women, or for any other god, for he will boast that he is greater than them all. Instead of these, he will worship the god of fortresses - a god his ancestors never knew - and lavish on him gold, silver, precious stones, and costly gifts." **Daniel 11:37-38**

"They worshiped the dragon for giving the beast such power, and they worshiped the beast.'Is there anyone as great as the beast?' they exclaimed.'Who is able to fight against him?'" **Revelation 13:4**

The Antichrist will only acknowledge one power, a military power he possesses. His power will be so great the people of the world will marvel in wonder and worship it, asking the rhetorical question of who among them is able to fight against his mighty kingdom.

The Descendants of Ishmael

His Life

In addition to various aspects of his character, the Bible provides us with numerous details concerning the life events and career of this man of lawlessness, beginning with his meteoric rise to fame from among ten kings.

Rises From Among 10 Kings

"It was different from any of the other beasts, and it had ten horns. As I was looking at the horns, suddenly another small horn appeared among them." **Daniel 7:7-8**

"His ten horns are ten kings who have not yet risen to power; they will be appointed to their kingdoms for one brief moment to reign with the beast. They will all agree to give their power and authority to him." **Revelation 17:12-13**

Ten kings will give their power and national sovereignty to the revived Roman Empire. From among them, the Antichrist will appear, and he will become the preeminent ruler among them.

Subdues 3 of the 10 Kings

"Three of the first horns were wrenched out, roots and all, to make room for it." **Daniel 7:8**

Apparently, three of the ten kings will oppose the Antichrist and his brazen grab for power. In the struggle that ensues, he will defeat them, and his control over the new Rome will become absolute.

7 Year Treaty with Israel

"He will make a treaty with the people for a period of one set of seven" **Daniel 9:27**

The Antichrist will make a treaty with the people of Israel for a period of seven years. The details and nature of this treaty are yet unknown, but many have speculated that in a bid for Middle Eastern peace, Israel will agree to rely on the Antichrist for its national defense.

He Will Conquer Many

Revelation Chapter 6 describes the Antichrist as a great conqueror riding on a white horse. He goes out to conquer many, and he wields a great sword. In his conquest, he will kill a sizeable portion of the world's population.

Will Rule Politically, Religiously, and Economically

"He exercised all the authority of the first beast. And he required all the earth and those who belong to this world to worship the first beast, who's death-wound had been healed." **Revelation 13:12** The Antichrist will exercise all the authority of the first beast, which is the revived Roman Empire. He will require the world to worship and give allegiance to this empire, which will be resurrected from the dustbin of history. "And he was given authority to rule over every tribe and people and language and nation." **Revelation 13:7** Not one person will escape the reach of the Antichrist and his governmental dominion.

"He required everyone - great and small, rich and poor, slave and free - to be given a <u>mark on the right hand or on the forehead</u>. And no one could buy or sell anything without that mark, which was either the name of the beast or the number representing his name." **Revelation 13:16-17**

The Antichrist will have unprecedented control over the world's financial transactions. He will have so much power that he will be able to determine on a case-by-case basis which individuals will be allowed to buy or sell *anything*.

Unprecedented Destruction

In his insatiable quest for personal glory, the Antichrist will cause an unprecedented amount of destruction. "He will become very strong, but not by his own power. He will cause a shocking amount of destruction and succeed in everything he does." **Daniel 8:24**

<u>**Abomination of Desolation**</u>

Jesus prophesied of a time of great tribulation, such as the world had never seen, nor ever will see again. He said this time period will begin with the desecration of the Jewish Temple:

"The time will come when you will see what Daniel the prophet spoke about: the sacrilegious object that causes desecration standing in the Holy Place." **Matthew 24:16**

The Antichrist will fulfill this prophesy by standing in the Jewish Temple and proclaiming himself to be God. He will set up an image in the Holy Place and demand the world worship it. "He will put an end to the sacrifices and offerings. Then as a climax to all his terrible deeds, he will set up a sacrilegious object that causes desecration, until the end that has been decreed is poured out on this defiler." **Daniel 9:27**

"He will exalt himself and defy every god there is and tear down every object of adoration and worship. He will position himself in the temple of God, claiming that he himself is God." **2 Thessalonians 2:4**

Destroys All Religion But His Own

The Book of Revelation describes the revived Roman Empire as being dominated by a prostitute. This prostitute symbolizes idolatrous religion, and although Satan loves idolatry, in the end time he will only tolerate worship of himself. As a result, it will become state policy of the revived Roman Empire to destroy all religion with the exception of worship of the dragon. "The scarlet beast and his ten horns - which represent ten kings who will reign with him - all hate the prostitute. They will strip her naked, eat her flesh, and burn her remains with fire." **Revelation 17:16**

Wages War Against the Saints

As part of his campaign to create universal worship of himself, the Antichrist will set out to destroy those who are faithful to God and His Son, Jesus Christ. "And the beast was allowed to wage war against God's holy people and overcome them." **Revelation 13:7**

"He will destroy powerful leaders and devastate the holy people. He will be a master of deception, defeating many by catching them off guard. Without warning he will destroy them. He will even take on the Prince of princes in battle, but he will be broken, though not by human power." **Daniel 8:24-25**

Kills Two-Thirds of the Jewish People

In his rage against the Jewish people, the Antichrist will manage to kill two-thirds of the Jewish race.

"Two-thirds of the people in the land will be cut off and die, says the Lord. But a third will be left in the land." **Zechariah 13:8-9**

Wages War Against Jesus Christ

In his arrogance, the Antichrist will lead a rebellion against Jesus Christ, and gather the world's armies to wage battle against the Lord and his heavenly armies. "He will even take on the Prince of princes in battle." **Daniel 8:25**

"And I saw three evil spirits that looked like frogs leap from the mouth of the dragon, the beast, and the false prophet. These miracle-working demons caused all the rulers of the world to gather for battle against the Lord on that great judgment day of God Almighty." **Revelation 16:13-14**

His Ultimate Destruction

Despite his worldly success, the reign of the Antichrist will be relatively brief - no more than seven years. Ultimately, he will be held accountable for his actions, and he will face the wrath of the Lamb of God, Jesus Christ.

Camps at Armageddon

While gathering the armies of the world to Jerusalem to wage battle against the Lord, the Antichrist will set up his camp and gather his armies in a place called Armageddon, the modern day city of Megiddo, Israel.

"He will halt between the glorious holy mountain and the sea and will pitch his royal tents there, but while he is there, his time will suddenly run out, and there will be no one to help him." **Daniel 11:45**

"And they gathered all the rulers and their armies to a place called Armageddon in Hebrew." **Revelation 16:16**

Destroyed Forever

Despite his arrogant belief that he can defeat God, the ultimate fate of the Antichrist was determined long ago. He will be completely destroyed in a rout of epic proportions.

"But then the court will pass judgment, and all his power will be taken away and completely destroyed." **Daniel 7:26**

Lake of Fire

As a result of his defeat, the Antichrist will be cast into the lake of fire (traditionally known as "Hell") where he will be tormented day and night for all of eternity.

His kingdom will meet the same fate, and be replaced by the Lord's Millennial Kingdom which will bring long-sought peace on earth. "Both the beast and his false prophet were thrown alive into the lake of fire that burns with sulfur." **Revelation 19:20**

Jesus offered the world by Satan...

In studying the prophecies of the Antichrist, we would be wise to refer to the Book of Matthew, where Jesus is tempted in the desert prior to his ministry. Here, we get a firsthand view of the deal brokered between the Antichrist and Satan: "Next the Devil took him to the peak of a very high mountain and showed him the nations of the world and all their glory.'I will give it all to you,' he said, 'if you will only kneel down and worship me.' 'Get out of here, Satan,' Jesus told him. 'For the scriptures say, 'You must worship the Lord your God; serve only him.' Then the Devil went away, and angels came and cared for Jesus." **Matthew 4:8-11**. Because He is faithful and true, Jesus turned down the Devil's offer to rule the kingdoms of the world. However, at some point in the future, a man will arise who will accept this deal with the Devil. He will sell his soul for a brief and destructive career as the most powerful dictator in human history. He will hold absolute power, and he will be the personification of all evil. But his destruction is certain. He challenges the Prince of Peace, and guess what? Victory is our:

"LORD AND SAVIOR JESUS CHRIST"!!!!!!

CHAPTER V

JIHAD

What Jihad IS NOT!

If you open a modern Oxford English dictionary, you would probably

find the definition of Jihad as "a holy war undertaken by Muslims against

non-believers". This is **a very poor definition.** Before trying to define what

Jihad is we should first define what it is NOT.

Jihad is **NOT** Holy War

Jihad is **NOT** blowing up one's self (Suicide is a sin in Islam)

A Prophet said, "Whoever intentionally swears falsely by a religion other than Islam, then he is what he has said, (if he says, 'If such thing is not true then I am a Jew,' he is really a Jew). And whoever commits suicide with piece of iron will be punished with the same piece of iron in the Hell Fire."A Prophet said, "A man was inflicted with wounds and he committed suicide, and so Allah said: My slave has caused death on himself hurriedly, so I forbid Paradise for him."

Jihad is **NOT** killing innocent people, Jihad is **NOT** flying a plane into a building packed with civilians

Jihad is **NOT** fighting out of anger and hatred

Jihad is **NOT** killing others just because they don't agree with you

Jihad is **NOT** killing others just because they are not Muslims

The real meaning of Jihad

Jihad is an Arabic word from the root Jee Ha Da. It literally means to struggle or strive. Jihad is struggling or striving in the way or sake of Allah. Jihad takes a very important status in the doctrine of Islam and is one of the basic duties for every Muslim. Though, it has nothing whatsoever to do with the term Holy War. Such a term, or its equivalent doesn't exist in the Islamic doctrine. The Christian Crusaders in the mid-ages invented this ideology of Holy War. There is nothing "Holy" about wars. Wars only involve killings and disasters!

Jihad has many forms,

- Jihad of the heart/soul (jihad bin nafs/qalb)
- Jihad by the tongue (jihad bil lisan)
- Jihad by the pen/knowledge (jihad bil qalam/ilm)
- Jihad by the hand (jihad bil yad)
- Jihad by the sword (jihad bis saif)

JIHAD

Jihad of the Heart/Soul

Jihad of the heart/soul; in Arabic: jihad bin nafs/qalb. It is referred as "**the greater Jihad**" (al-jihad al-akbar). It is one's inner struggle of good against evil; refraining oneself from the whispers of Shaitan (Satan). This process involves allowing Islam to transform one's soul to achieving internal peace; and forgoing the hatred and anger. "Jihad is ordained for you (Muslims) though you dislike it, and it may be that you dislike a thing which is good for you and that you like a thing which is bad for you. Allah knows but you do not know."

{Quran, Surah 2: Al-Baqarah, Verse 216; Mohsin Translation}

Jihad by the tongue

Jihad by the tongue; in Arabic: jihad bil lisan. It is defending Islam and spreading Islam by scholarly lectures, speeches and debates. It often overlaps with Da'awah (invitation to Islam, or spreading the message of Islam). In The Last Sermon, Prophet Mohammed (peace be upon him) asked the listeners whether he has passed on the message to them; and they confirmed affirmatively. Then the Messenger of Allah ordered all those present today to pass on the same message to those who are not here today; and the last person to hear the message should understand it better than the people here.

Jihad by the pen/knowledge

Jihad by the pen/knowledge; in Arabic: jihad bil qalam/ilm. This form of Jihad involves scholarly research of Islam in aiding the spread and defense of Islam; and publishing written articles in clearing misconceptions and correction lies against Islam. Examples of such Jihad include the research and discovery of scientific evidences, literature miracles and mathematical miracles from the Quran. Messenger of Allah once stated that the ink of a scholar is holier than the blood of a martyr; and one who is reading looks handsome in front of Allah.

Jihad by the hand

Jihad by the hand; in Arabic: jihad bil yad. This is a Jihad of action rather than words. At certain areas, it overlaps with Zakart (charity) and Hajj (pilgrimage). Some of its examples include giving charity to the poor and needy, performing Hajj or Ummrah, helping those who need help, saving people's lives, etc. These are more of physical deeds instead of words. "A person whose feet become dust ridden because of [striving] in the way of Allah will never be touched by the flames of Hell" { Sahih Bukhari 2811} The most beautiful of all Jihad is a perfect Hajj. It involves testing of one's patience and piety to the apex. The whole period of Hajj, with just one intention and aim, worshiping Allah!

JIHAD

Jihad by the sword

Jihad by the sword; in Arabic: jihad bis saif. In contrary to Jihad of the heart/soul; this form of Jihad is referred as **"the lesser jihad"** (al-jihad alasghar). Sometimes it is necessary to undertake Jihad by the sword. This would include usage of arsenals and engaging in a combat. This could be simply a bunch of freedom fighters or an organized campaign of army. Jihad by the sword is use of arms to engage into a combat. It is **not** misuse of arms to create violence. There are only two situations were Jihad by the sword is allowed to be undertaken. 1) **For self-defense,** When someone attacks you or when your nation has been attacked, engaging into combat due to self defense.

2) **Fighting against evil and unjust,** It is also a sin if a Muslim sees unjust been done, capable of stopping it, yet not doing anything about it. This can include war on drug, war on child labor as well as war on terror! The American administration today seems to be launching a global war on terror, but are they the first to launch the war on terror? The Muslims already announced the war on terror fourteen centuries ago, under the name of Jihad bis saif! There are many rules and limitations when engaging in combat under the title of Jihad. For example, civilians are not to be harmed; trees are not to be cut down; asylum should be granted to surrendering enemy soldiers. "And if anyone of the Mushrikun seeks your protection then grant him protection, so that he may hear the Word of Allah, and then

escort him to where he can be secure, that is because they are men who know not." {Quran, Surah 9: At-Taubah, Verse 6; Mohsin Translation} The above verse states that when an enemy soldier surrenders during a battle, the Muslim soldiers must grant asylum and in addition, escort him to safety! The treatment for prisoners of war is also clearly stated in the Quran. Prisoners of war under Muslim prisons are to eat, drink and dress the same Muslim soldiers eat, drink and dress. And even under the unfortunate event of shortage of food, it is the prisoners who are to eat first before the Muslim soldiers guarding them!

A closer look at the Sword

Despite the fact that Jihad by the sword is the lesser Jihad, it is the only form of Jihad that most of the people in the world perceive Jihad as. This is unfortunate, especially for the Muslims. Many so-called "teachers of Islam" have been misusing this to assemble their so-called "holy army" to fight their so-called "holy war". But you can't blame the religion for what a few of its people do. In every society, there is a black sheep. Self-Defense:

Since Jihad by the sword has been overwhelmingly magnified in the wrong angle, let's take a closer look at it in the right angle. **What is wrong with Jihad by the sword if it is fighting for self-defense?** In the early years of revelation of Islam in Mecca, Muslims were not granted permission from Allah to fight.

JIHAD

So the Muslims suffered both moral and physical humiliations from the non-Muslims in Mecca. The first verses regarding Jihad were then revealed allowing Muslims to undertake self-defense. "And fight in the Way of Allah those who fight you, but transgress not the limits. Truly, Allah likes not the transgressors. {Quran, Surah 2: Al-Baqarah, Verse 190; Mohsin Translation} Many of the Quranic verses are being quoted out of context to wrongly justify terrorist actions. Yet, most of those verses are only referring to a particular situation; such as Battle of Badr or Battle of Uhud. Intention and war against Satan: "Those who believe fight in the Cause of Allah, and those who disbelieve, fight in the cause of Satan. So fight against the friends of Satan. Ever feeble indeed is the plot of Satan." {Quran, Surah 4: An-Nisa, Verse 76; Mohsin Translation} Now the second question is **what is wrong in fighting against evil and liberating people from sufferings**? "Once a person came to the Prophet and said that some people fight for the spoils of war, some for fame and some to show off their valor; he then asked the Prophet: "Which one of them fights in the way of Allah". The Prophet replied: "Only that person fights in the way of Allah who sets foot in the battlefield to raise high the name of Allah". { Sahih Bukhari 2810}

Who is a Holy Warrior?

According to the Quran, a martyr who died in the way of Jihad is promised Paradise. But what are the criteria of martyr, or in other words, what are the criteria of a Holy Warrior undertaking the True Jihad? The most famous of all Hadith is the one regarding everything we do are judged by our intensions; so as it is mentioned in the previous chapter. So who is an example of a Holy Warrior? Ali bin Abu Talib, cousin of Prophet Mohammed and the fourth Caliph of the Islamic Ummah is a good example. During one of the battles, Ali was about to give a deathblow to an enemy soldier. Just then, that enemy soldier spat at Ali. Ali then suddenly stopped, threw down his sword and refused to kill that enemy soldier. After the battle, Ali's soldiers asked Ali why he suddenly stopped and refused to kill that enemy soldier on the battlefield. Ali explained that he got angry when that enemy soldier spat at him. So if he had killed that enemy soldier right then, he would be killing out of his own anger and no longer fighting for Justice. In the sight of Allah, he would then be no different from a murderer. Brothers and Sisters that is how we should see a Holy Warrior!

CHAPTER VI

Death in the Name of GOD

Our Lord Jesus, by giving his disciples notice of trouble, designed that the terror might not be a surprise to them. It is possible for those who are real enemies to God's service, to pretend zeal for it. This does not lessen the sin of the persecutors; villanies will never be changed by putting the name of God to them. As Jesus in his sufferings, so his followers in theirs should look to the fulfilling of Scripture. He did not tell them sooner, because he was with them to teach, guide, and comfort them; they needed not then this promise of the Holy Spirit's presence. It will silence us to ask, Whence troubles come? It will satisfy us to ask, Where they go? for we know they work for good. It is the common fault and folly of melancholy Christians to look only on the dark side of the cloud, and to turn a deaf ear to the voice of joy and gladness. That, which filled the disciples' hearts with sorrow, was too great affection for this present life. Nothing more hinders our joy in God, than the love of the world, and the sorrow of the world which comes from it. Out of the synagogues - See the notes at John 9:22. They would excommunicate them from their religious assemblies. This was often done. Compare Acts 6:13-14; Acts 9:23-24; Acts 17:5; Acts 21:27-31. Whosoever kills you - This refers principally to the Jews. It is also true of the Gentiles, that in their persecution of Christians they supposed they were rendering acceptable service to their gods. God's service - The Jews who persecuted the apostles regarded them as blasphemers, and as seeking to overthrow the temple service, and the system of religion which God had established. Thus, they supposed they were rendering service to God in putting them to death, Acts 6:13-14; Acts 21:28-31. Sinners, especially hypocrites, often cloak enormous crimes under the pretence of great zeal for religion. Men often suppose, or profess to suppose, that they are rendering God service when they persecute others; and, under the pretence of great zeal for truth and purity, evince all possible bigotry, pride, malice, and uncharitableness. The people of God have suffered most from those who have been conscientious persecutors; and some of the most malignant foes which true Christians have ever had have been in the church, and have been professed ministers of the gospel, persecuting them under pretence of great zeal for the cause of purity and religion. It is no evidence of piety that a man is full of zeal against those whom he supposes to be heretics; and it is one of the best proofs that a man knows nothing of the religion of Jesus when he is eminent for self-conceit in his own views of orthodoxy, and firmly fixed in the opinion that all who differ from him and his sect must of course be wrong. 2. They shall put you out of the synagogue—(John 9:22; 12:42). The time comes, that whosoever kills you will think that he doeth God service—The words mean religious service—"that he is offering a service to God." (So Saul of Tarsus, Ga 1:13, 14; Php 3:6). The term synagogue, as it is used often in Scripture to signify those places of public worship which they had in country towns and cities, is proper to the Jews; but as it signified an assembly of people met together in any place, it as well agreed to other people as to them. Our Lord here, in pursuit of the argument which he hath been upon from John 15:18, forewarns his disciples, that when he should be taken from them, the Jews first should excommunicate them as heretics, or schismatics: and I know not why what our Savior here said may not also be extended as a prophecy of what has since been done and is yet doing under the tyranny of the pope. As also the latter clause, which, though at first applicable to the Jews, who stoned Stephen upon a charge of blasphemy, in which it is apparent that they thought they did God good service, and doubtless slew many others; yet certainly it also referred to others, even as many as shall do the same thing to the end of the world. They shall put you out of the synagogues ... The Jews had made a law already, that he that confessed that Jesus was the Messiah, should be cast out of their synagogues; and they had put it in execution upon the blind man Christ restored to sight, for his profession of faith in him; which struck such a terror upon the people, that even many of the chief rulers who believed that Jesus was the true Messiah, durst not confess him, because of this law; for it was what they could not bear the thoughts of, to be deemed and treated as heretics and apostates, and the vilest of wretches: for this putting out of the synagogue, was not the lesser excommunication, which was called "Niddui", and was a "separation" from a particular synagogue for a while; but the greater excommunication, either by "Cherem", or "Shammatha"; when a person was cut out from the whole body of the Jewish church, called often the synagogue, or congregation of the people; and was devoted and consigned to utter destruction, which was the height of their ecclesiastical power, their rage and malice could carry them to; and this the apostles were to expect; nay, not only this, but to have their lives taken away by ruffians, under pretence of zeal for the service of God, and interest of religion: yea, the time cometh, that whosoever killed you, will think that he doth God service. For this is not to be understood of their being delivered up into the hands of civil magistrates, and of their being tried, judged, condemned, and put to death by their orders, but of their being murdered by a set of men called "zealots"; who, in imitation of Phinehas, as they pretended, took upon them, whenever they found any person guilty of a capital crime, as idolatry, blasphemy, or what they judged so, to fall upon him at once, and without any more ado kill him; nor were they accountable to any court of judicature for such an action, and which was reckoned laudable and praiseworthy: in this way, and by the hands of such miscreants, Stephen the protomartyr lost his life; for though they had him before a council, and suborned witnesses against him, yet when in his own defense he said what these "zealots" interpreted blasphemy, they ran upon him at once, and cast him out of the city, and stoned him to death; and without any leave or authority from the Sanhedrim, as appears: and these men were accounted good men, zealous "with a zeal for God", his honor and glory; and valued themselves much upon such butcheries and inhumanity, and thought, as our Lord here says, that they "did God service"; or as the Syriac renders it, , "offered a sacrifice to God", and so the Arabic and Ethiopic: and indeed this is a rule the Jews, and which they form upon the instance and example of Phinehas;"that whoever sheds the blood of wicked men, (and such they reckoned the apostles and followers of Christ to be,), "it is all one as if he offered a sacrifice";" they looked upon this to be a sacrifice acceptable and well pleasing to God: so the Apostle Paul, in his unregenerate state, thought he ought to do many things contrary to the name of Christ: and that he was doing God service, when he prosecuted the church, and gave his voice with these ruffians, to put the saints to death.

CHAPTER VII

Where there is Peace & Safety Disaster Strikes

1 Thessalonians 5:3...

The Day of the Lord

<u>1</u>Now, brothers and sisters, about times and dates we do not need to write to you, <u>2</u>for you know very well that the day of the Lord will come like a thief in the night. <u>3</u>While people are saying, "Peace and safety," destruction will come on them suddenly, as labor pains on a pregnant woman, and they will not escape. <u>4</u>But you, brothers and sisters, are not in darkness so that this day should surprise you like a thief. <u>5</u>You are all children of the light and children of the day. We do not belong to the night or to the darkness. <u>6</u>So then, let us not be like others, who are asleep, but let us be awake and sober. <u>7</u>For those who sleep, sleep at night, and those who get drunk, get drunk at night. <u>8</u>But since we belong to the day, let us be sober, putting on faith and love as a breastplate, and the hope of salvation as a helmet. <u>9</u>For God did not appoint us to suffer wrath but to receive salvation through our Lord Jesus Christ. <u>10</u>He died for us so that, whether we are awake or asleep, we may live together with him. <u>11</u>Therefore encourage one another and build each other up, just as in fact you are doing. It is needless or useless to ask about the particular time of Christ's coming. Christ did not reveal this to the apostles.

The Descendants of Ishmael

There are times and seasons for us to work in and these are our duty and interest to know and observe; but as to the time when we must give up our account, we know it not, nor is it needful that we should. The coming of Christ will be a great surprise to men. Our Lord himself said so. As the hour of death is the same to each person that the judgment will be to mankind in general, so the same remarks answer for both. Christ's coming will be terrible to the ungodly. Their destruction will overtake them while they dream of happiness, and please themselves with vain amusements. There will be no means to escape the terror or the punishment of that day. This day will be a happy day to the righteous. They are not in darkness; they are the children of the light. It is the happy condition of all true Christians. But how many are speaking peace and safety to themselves, over whose heads utter destruction is hovering! Let us endeavor to awaken ourselves and each other, and guard against our spiritual enemies. For when they shall say, Peace and safety - That is, when the wicked shall say this, for the apostle here refers only to those on whom "sudden destruction" will come; compare Matthew 24:36-42 ; 2 Peter 3:3-4....that when the Lord Jesus shall come, the world will not all be converted. There will be some to be "destroyed." How large this proportion will be, it is impossible now to ascertain. This supposition, however, is not inconsistent with the belief that there will be a general prevalence of the gospel before that period the impenitent and wicked world... (ISIS...Al Qaeda...etc) will be sunk in carnal security when he comes.

Where there is Peace & Safety Disaster Strikes

They will regard themselves as safe. They will see no danger. They will give no heed to warning. They will be unprepared for his advent. So it has always been. it seems to be a universal truth in regard to all the visitations of God to wicked people for punishment, that he comes upon them at a time when they are not expecting him, and that they have no faith in the predictions of his advent. So it was in the time of the flood; in the destruction of Sodom Gomorrah, and Jerusalem; in the overthrow of Babylon: so it is when the sinner dies, and so it will be when the Lord Jesus shall return to judge the world. One of the most remarkable facts about the history of man is that he takes no warning from his Maker; he never changes his plans, or feels any emotion, because his Creator "thunders damnation along his path," and threatens to destroy him in hell. Sudden destruction - Destruction that was unforeseen or unexpected. The word here rendered "sudden," occurs nowhere else in the New Testament, except in Luke 21:34, "Lest that day come upon you unawares." The word rendered "destruction" - occurs in the New Testament only here and in 1 Corinthians 5:5; 2 Thessalonians 1:9; 1 Timothy 6:9, in all of which places it is correctly translated destruction. The word destruction is familiar to us. It means, properly, demolition; pulling down; the annihilation of the form of anything, or that form of parts which constitutes it what it is; as the destruction of grass by eating; of a forest by cutting down the trees; of life by murder; of the soul by consigning it to misery. It does not necessarily mean annihilation - for a house or city is not annihilated which is pulled down or burnt; a forest is not annihilated which is cut down;

and a man is not annihilated whose character and happiness are destroyed. In regard to the destruction here referred to, we may remark:

it will be after the return of the Lord Jesus to judgment; and hence it is not true that the wicked experience all the punishment which they ever will in the present life; that it seems fairly implied that the destruction which they will then suffer will not be annihilation, but will be connected with conscious existence; and, that they will then be cut off from life and hope and salvation. How can the solemn affirmations that they will be "destroyed suddenly," be consistent with the belief that all people will be saved? Is it the same thing to be destroyed and to be saved? Does the Lord Jesus, when he speaks of the salvation of his people, say that he comes to destroy them? As travail upon a woman with child - This expression is sometimes used to denote great consternation, as in Psalm 48:6; Jeremiah 6:24; Micah 4:9-10; great pain, as Isaiah 53:11; Jeremiah 4:31; John 16:21; or the suddenness with which anything occurs; Jeremiah 13:21. It seems here to be used to denote two things; first, that the coming of the Lord to a wicked world will be sudden; and, secondly, that it will be an event of the most distressing and overwhelming nature. And they shall not escape - That is, the destruction, or punishment. They calculated on impunity, but now the time will have come when none of these refuges will avail them, and no rocks will cover them from the "wrath to come."

The Kingdom Culture Ministries
&
Christian Self Publishing's

THE KINGDOM CULTURE   EXPLORATORY

STUDY BIBLE

www.ingramcontent.com/pod-product-compliance
Lightning Source LLC
Chambersburg PA
CBHW022106160426
43198CB00008B/374